PROLIFERATION

Heaven's Blueprint for Multiplication
expansion and Dominion

DAVID S. PHILEMON

Royal Diadem Publishing INC

Book Title: PROLIFERATION
Author: DAVID S. PHILEMON
Phone Number: +1773 521 3954
Email Address: info.royaldiadempublishing@gmail.com

This book was designed and published by:

Royal Diadem Publishing INC
⬡ info.royaldiadempublishing@gmail.com
☏ +1773 521 3954

All scripture quoted are taken from King James Version of the Bible

Dedication

I dedicate this book to the King of kings and Lord of lords, Jesus Christ whose Kingdom is ever increasing and whose glory fills the earth. To my children, both biological and spiritual you are living testimonies of God's power to multiply, expand, and establish His dominion on the earth.
And to you, the reader receive this not just as a book, but as a prophetic impartation. May these words awaken the seeds God has placed within you, cause them to multiply beyond measure, expand your territory, and position you to walk boldly in Kingdom dominion. Your season of proliferation begins now, in Jesus' name!
With faith and expectation,

Apostle Dr. David Philemon

ACKNOWLEDGEMENT

his book would not have been possible without the unwavering support, dedication, and talent of an extraordinary team. My deepest gratitude goes to each of you for your contributions, insights, and encouragement throughout this journey.

First and foremost, thank you to Rev. Mimi Philemon, my dear wife; my brother-in-law, Rev. Shina Gentry; my Assistant Pastor, Rev. Bright Amudoaghan; and the Lead Pastor of Church on Fire International, Pastor Peculiar Onyekere, for your incredible effort, encouragement, and steadfast belief in this project. Your support has been instrumental in bringing this vision to life.

To the dedicated leaders of Royal Diadem Publishing, Ide Imogie and Kishawna Bailey, I am immensely grateful for believing in this project from the very beginning and for investing your time and energy into its development. Your creativity, dedication, and expertise have been the backbone of this endeavor.

I am especially thankful to the entire Royal Diadem Publishing team for your meticulous attention to detail, refining every page, and ensuring that each word reflects our shared vision.

A heartfelt thank you to my family, friends, and colleagues, whose unwavering encouragement and faith in this work gave me the courage and strength to see it through.

Finally, to all the readers and supporters who give meaning to these pages thank you. I am humbled and honored to share this journey with each of you.
With all my gratitude, David Philemon

Special Call To Salvation & New Beginnings From Apostle Dr. David Philemon

Dear Beloved, You are not reading this by accident God Himself has led you here because He loves you more than you could ever imagine. No matter where you've been, what you've done, or how far you feel from Him, His arms are open wide to receive you today.

The Bible says in John 3:16: *"For God so loved the world that He gave His one and only Son, that whoever believes in Him shall not perish but have eternal life."* That means you. Jesus Christ came to take away your sins, heal your heart, and give you a brand-new life one filled with peace, purpose, and hope.

Today, you can step into that new life. If you are ready to surrender to Him, pray this from your heart:

The Salvation Prayer Heavenly Father, I come to You in the name of Jesus. I confess that I am a sinner in need of Your mercy. I believe that Jesus Christ is Your Son, that He died on the cross for my sins, and that You raised Him from the dead. Today, I turn away from my old life and give You my whole heart. Jesus, come into my life. Be my Lord, my Savior, and my best friend. Wash me clean, fill me with Your Holy Spirit, and guide me into the life You created me to live. Thank You, Father, for loving me, forgiving me, and making me Yours. In Jesus' name, Amen.

Welcome to the Family of God! If you prayed that prayer with faith, congratulations! Your sins are forgiven, your name is written in the Book of Life, and heaven is celebrating you right now. This is the beginning of the greatest journey you will ever take and you are not alone.

Your Next Steps:

* Connect with a Bible-believing church: You were never meant to

walk this journey alone.

* Read God's Word daily: The Bible will show you who God is and who you are in Him.

* Pray often: Talk to God about everything. He delights in hearing your voice.

* Share your testimony: Let others know what God has done for you.

Your life will never be the same again. God's plans for you are greater than you can imagine so walk forward in faith, knowing He is with you every step of the way.

CONTENTS

INTRODUCTION

Do you know that it is an aberration, a complete abnormality, and outside of God's glorious intention for a child of God, who is a partaker of the blessings made available through the sacrifice of Christ, to be found in want, lack, sadness, rejection, depression, beaten down, and broken? This is not God's plan for His people; in fact, it is far from it! God's design for His children is abundance, growth, and flourishing in every area of life, so even before we go deeper, I want you to know that anything contrary to this is outside of His divine blueprint. However, the acceptable path for a believer, according to Scripture, is that though you may start small, you are not permitted to remain small, instead you are to increase. Job 8:7 puts it this way

> *"Though thy beginning was small, yet thy latter end should greatly increase."*

This is God's design, it is a plan of progress, increase, and expansion in all spheres of life in a rapid successive way.

Stagnation, barrenness, and lack are not in any way near His plan for your life because as a child of God, you are called to bring forth results in rapid succession. You must grow, thrive, and multiply, just as God's blessing commands.

This intention of God is even revealed from the beginning because in Genesis 1:28, you will see that He said, *"Be fruitful, and multiply, and replenish the earth, and subdue it: and have dominion..."* This is a command; it is not just a suggestion; it is a divine mandate! Can't you see that you have been "blessed to proliferate," bringing forth results, multiplying, and dominating?

Suppose you cannot lay hold of this revelation about God's intention for your life. In that case, the enemy will take advantage of your ignorance and make a public spectacle of you because a lack of understanding that brings light is what keeps many believers limited, frustrated, and stuck in cycles of failure, when they are destined for greatness. Hosea 4:6: *"My people are destroyed for lack of knowledge."* Ignorance is indeed a dangerous thing, especially when it comes to God's principles for success. He desires that you do not remain small but grow in every area, spiritually, financially, emotionally, and relationally. You were never meant to live a life of mediocrity. God wants you to rise from glory to glory, and you must know it.

Now, there's so much that the Lord will be revealing to you as you read through the pages of this book. Do not just read it casually; do it with a prayerful heart, a focused spirit, and a determination to see the blessings of God overflowing in your life. Understand that the life of a believer is designed for continual increase, and that is what God has planned for you.

If you feel stuck, minor, or frustrated, you should know that it is not too late; God is ready to turn your story around. The keys and principles that will unlock this rapid increase in your life are embedded in the truths of God's Word, and by His grace, he has revealed them in this book you are now holding.

The principles you are about to discover will show you how to unlock divine blessings, honour, glory and power, and this is not just about hoping for better days but about positioning yourself for the rapid successions of blessings that God has already ordained for you.

So, get ready!

The time for your manifestation is here.

The time for stagnation is over!

The enemy has tried to limit you, but God is setting you up for greatness!

CHAPTER ONE

THE TRUE BLESSINGS OF GOD

◆ ◆ ◆

"God's blessings do not just wish you well; they empower you to thrive, open doors, and shape your destiny."

◆ ◆ ◆

Empowered To Flourish

Understanding The True Meaning Of Blessings

The Bible says in Job 8:7, *"Though thy beginning was small, yet thy latter end should greatly increase."* Now, focus on that powerful word *"yet."* It is a divine turning point, ushering in a promise of supernatural increase! Know this: the primary assignment of God's blessing upon your life is to beautify your latter end. And what is your latter end, you may ask. Your latter end is not some distant future somewhere; Your latter end is the very next minute after this one! It is every moment from now onwards, stretching into eternity, and the blessings of the Lord, which we are talking about, are already working in your life and causing your life to increase, not just in any direction, but in the right direction.

What do I mean by the *"right direction"*? I am talking about the most favorable path to you and, most importantly, brings honor to our God. When you begin to experience advancement in this right direction, it brings great pleasure to the heart of our Father. Why? Because His ultimate goal for you is constant improvement, progress, and continual increase. The Lord truly wants you to improve with each passing day. This is why he declared in Job 8 that even if you start with little, the "blessing" empowers you to end with much! Declare it loud, "I will end with much because I am blessed!" Now, I need you to keep these words in your heart even as you read on, let them continually resonate in your spirit, and take root in your heart.

The Message translation wonderfully puts the same Job 8:7 by saying,

> *"Even though you are not much right now, you will end up better."*

Child of God, things may not exactly be what you want now, but it is time for your faith to rise because you will end up better than you could ever imagine! Do you see the power in these words? The blessing of God has already predicted and prophesied your glorious end; this is not just a mere possibility; it is a divine decree spoken over your life.

Pray this prayer with a sincere heart whole of faith and trust in God: *"My Father, in the name of Jesus, by Your mercy, Your power, and Your authority, I engage the power of the blessing! I apply the blessing to every department of my life and command increase for Your honor and Your Kingdom!"*

Now, when I talk about "the blessing," I know many people out there probably have a wrong concept about it because of the way the word has been bacterized, trivialized, and taken for granted in the world today. If, for example, I say, *"You are blessed,"* I want you to know that it is not just a casual greeting or a religious cliché; it is a potent and life-altering force that has been tragically misunderstood in our modern world. For so many people the word 'blessing' has been so overused that it now means nothing to them when they hear it. Just walk around the streets a bit, and you will hear people keep using phrases like *"bless you," "blessings,"* and *"blessings, bro"* without truly understanding the weight of what they are saying. But I tell you today, when the *"blessing"* is properly understood and applied, it becomes a catalyst for unprecedented growth and progress in your life because the *"blessing"* of God is not impotent; it is we who have diluted its power through our lack of understanding. Until it comes from the heart, saying to someone, *"I bless you,"* cannot affect your world and your environment.

If you are not careful, you will miss out on many opportunities to be blessed because you have been declaring *"blessings"* without genuinely meaning it or even comprehending the significance of your actions. This is a dangerous trap, and the reason you will miss out on many blessings is that when the proper authority, probably your prophet of God, a pastor, or a person walking in their God-given anointing pronounces God's blessings over your life, you may just dismiss it as another casual greeting as you have been greeting people. And in doing so, you may miss a life-altering moment that the Lord has ordained for your benefit right from the foundations of the world.

Let us clarify this: when your friend says, *"Good morning,"* it is a polite greeting, but when your prophet declares, *"Good morning,"* it is a powerful prophecy! Do you see the difference? Your friend might say, *"Blessings,"* and it is just a well-wish, but when God's spiritual authority over your life says, *"Blessings,"* then you should immediately start dancing because that's a declaration that has the power to shape your entire destiny and even your generations to come.

Yes! One word of blessing from the right source can determine the entire trajectory of your life, it can open doors that were previously shut, break chains that have held you back, and usher you into a season of unprecedented favor and increase. So I implore you, do not take the *"blessing"* lightly. You must learn to treat it with the reverence and respect it deserves. When you hear a word of blessing pronounced over your life, receive it with faith and expectation, let it sink deep into your spirit, and let it begin to transform your reality.

These are not just sentiments and so you must be careful, there are many who missed their moments of great change just by this simple mistake. God wants to revolutionize every aspect of your existence through his blessings.

God's blessings are his empowerment over your life, His divine license, and supernatural help, all working on your behalf to elevate you to heights you never thought possible and heights you will never be able to achieve in your own strength.

Altar Intelligence

The Spiritual Consequences Of Our Choices

Let me tell you about Esau who is perhaps the most foolish man to ever walk alongside greatness and yet end up in a miserable way. You see, Esau and Jacob must have had the incredible privilege of learning from their grandfather, Abraham, a man who walked closely with God, but when you study, the life of Esau from the Bible you will realize that he is a man who was always shortsighted, and because of this, we can be sure through is actions of selling his birthright for just a bowl of meal that he was a man who must have despised his grandfather's teachings and instructions.

Perhaps when Abraham would be lecturing him about God, in his heart he would be saying *"Grandpa, you are lecturing us about serving God? Give me a break! I have seen the mess in your own life. You had a child with Grandma's housemaid! How can you talk about God when you couldn't even keep your own house in order?"* But here's the critical lesson you must learn *"When an authority figure carries what your destiny requires, you must look beyond their imperfections and focus on the blessing they bear"* This is the only way you will be able to receive the blessings that are meant for you.

Let us illustrate this in a better way. Imagine your beloved grandmother suffering a heart attack and being rushed to the hospital, but then there are two doctors available. Let's say the first doctor is a very nice guy, very kind, and even a good Christian, but then he is not so skilled, in fact, his last two patients died. But then the second doctor is very mean, harsh, and lacks respect, and coupled with all these he even smokes and drinks. However, he is very skilled and everyone he operates on always survives and becomes better, who would you trust with your grandmother's life? The skilled doctor who can save her, even if he is very unpleasant, or the nice doctor who might be unable to help?

I am sure you would rather choose the one with the skill to save her life, wouldn't you? The same principle applies in the spiritual realm. Before someone becomes a spiritual authority, you should know that they have often weathered storms, faced failures, and learned to transform difficulties into stepping stones. This is what Esau should have realized in dealing with Abraham, rather than despise him. Because people who have been through so much and even made mistakes in life yet still emerged as victors truly have something your destiny desperately needs. Abraham was a man who walked with God for 24 long years before seeing the fulfillment of God's promise. Yes, he made a mistake with Hagar, but that error did not negate his miracle. Isaac, your father, Abraham would say, is living proof of God's faithfulness and my commitment to God.

But Esau, in his foolishness, had no regard for the *"blessing"* (the birthright and prophetic destiny of his lineage). Tragically, this disregard eventually caught up with him, and so when the time came for his father to bestow it on him, the spiritual patterns he had set in motion worked against him.

One thing you should know and never forget is that every action we take, every decision we make, and every word we speak sends a spiritual intelligence to our altar. The things you despise, ignore, or reject aren't simply forgotten in the spiritual realm; they go directly to your altar, declaring, *"This is the kind of life I desire."* So, Esau had already sent a clear message to his altar by despising his birthright and selling it to his younger brother. So, when the moment arrived for the blessing, his altar responded accordingly, and his brother Jacob received what was meant for him.

Understanding The Mystery Of Altar Intelligence

Can you imagine the anguish and sorrow that must have filled Esau's heart when he finally realized he needed *"the blessing"* to give meaning to his life? But by then, it was too late. I am sure by this time, all the teachings of Abraham suddenly began to make sense to him, but his altar was now working against him. What rightfully belonged to Him had already been transferred to Jacob because his altar had already received intelligence from his previous actions that he despised the blessing. Meanwhile, Jacob's altar was working in his favor because Jacob had fought and struggled to obtain that blessing; However, he resorted to deception, the spirit realm backed him up, because unlike Esau he had regard for *"the blessing"*.

The blessing is so potent that even a foolish man like Esau was brought to tears upon realizing its value too late. But now, let's dig deeper into altar intelligence. Do not forget, I said every decision we make, every action we take, and every word we speak sends a message to the spiritual realm; this is like we are constantly programming our personal spiritual computer, which is *"our altar,"* with the kind of life we want to live. What you need to realize here is that when Esau despised his birthright, he was not just making a poor decision; he was sending a powerful message to the spirit realm, saying, *"I do not value the spiritual inheritance prepared for me. I would rather have temporary satisfaction than a long-term blessing."* And his altar, faithful to the intelligence it received, acted accordingly when the time came for the blessing to be given.

Answer this? What have you been programming in your altar, what kinds of words have you been speaking, what kind of actions have you been taking? You may say, *"Hey, Sir, but I am not like Esau. I will never sell my birthright."* Are you sure? Do you not know each time you miss church for the sake of a movie; you are sending intelligence to your altar that you do not prioritize the blessings of God? Do you not know each time you choose the bed of sin rather than the bed of righteousness; you are sending a message to your altar that you do not prioritize God and His ways? It is straightforward to insult Esau, but when you examine your life, you will realize that you have been doing the same thing over and over again, always choosing temporary gratification, temporary pleasure, and temporary sin over your true birthright. It is time to repent now.

This is a deep spiritual principle that you must understand, our altars are not passive; they are active and responsive in such a way that they can release negative spirits or angelic beings either for our favor or disfavor; these spirits are meant to shape our lives destinies based on the intelligence we have been feeding them. So, if you consistently make choices in line with God's will and value His blessings, you are programming your altars to work in your favor, but when you consistently make choices that devalue spiritual things and prioritize temporary pleasures, you are programming your altar to work against you.

Every time you choose to pray instead of worry, you are sending intelligence to your altar that says, *"I trust in God's power more than my problems."* Every time you choose to forgive instead of holding a grudge, you are sending intelligence to your altar that says, *"I value God's grace and mercy."* Every time you choose to give generously instead of hoarding, you are sending intelligence to your altar that says, *"I believe in God's abundance and provision."* On the other side, every time you choose to worry instead of pray, to hold onto bitterness instead of forgiving, to be selfish instead of generous, you are sending negative intelligence to your altar. You are essentially telling your altar, *"This is the kind of person I want to be, this is the kind of life I want to live."*

And here's the crucial part, when the time comes for blessings to be released, when it is time for prayers to be answered, when it is time for breakthroughs to manifest, your altar will respond based on the wrong intelligence you have been feeding it with.

This principle applies to every area of our lives, the job promotion you are believing for, the healing you are praying for, the breakthrough in your ministry you are expecting, all of these are influenced by the intelligence you have been sending to your altar so you better be careful and make sure you are not destroying your life with your own hands.

Please do not neglect the instruction to examine your life, what kind of intelligence are you sending to your altar? Are your daily choices, your words, your actions, and your attitudes programming your altar for blessings or for curses? Are you, like Jacob, consistently demonstrating that you value God's blessings? Or are you, like Esau, carelessly disregarding the spiritual inheritance that has been prepared for you? Do not ever forget that your altar is always listening. Make sure you are sending the right messages because when the time comes for your blessing to be released, you want your altar working for you, not against you.

Blessed To Be A Blessing

The Responsibility Of God's Empowerment

Ponder deeply on this perplexing question: Why is it that so many individuals, despite receiving the blessings of the Almighty, continually struggles to truly benefit from them? The answer, I assure you, lies not in the potency of the blessing itself, but in our comprehension and application of it. The blessings of God on your life will always remain dormant and ineffective when you fail to understand its true nature and purpose. Yes! It is only when we fully understand the blessing that you can accurately be able to apply it to your life; and oh, when you use it correctly, that is when you will begin to witness the magnificent life-altering benefits that God intended for you all along.

Know that your Heavenly Father is deeply committed to your destiny and He is never content with you living a life of mediocrity or obscurity. No, His divine plan is to transform you into a voice that will resound through the corridors of time, a voice that will never be forgotten. And I prophesy that by the grace of God Almighty, you shall indeed become that voice, a beacon of hope and inspiration to generations yet unborn in the mighty name of Jesus.

Once again, what is this powerful gift called *"the blessing"* that has been bestowed upon us as children of God? To truly understand its magnitude, look at Genesis chapter 12, where we find the seminal moment of blessing in the life of Abraham, our father in faith. Genesis 12:1-3

> *"Now the Lord had said unto Abram, get thee out of thy country, and from thy kindred, and thy father's house, unto a land that I will shew thee: And I will make of thee a great nation, and I will bless thee, and make thy name*

great, and thou shalt be a blessing: And I will bless them that bless thee, and curse him that curseth thee: and in thee shall all families of the earth be blessed."

These words are not just ancient history; they are a living and breathing covenant that extends to us even today, when you understand this you will indeed be able to understand the divine destiny that God has prepared for each one of us.

Prophetic Words For America!

Let me share something with you, *I have been fervently interceding for North America, for I sense in my spirit that we are entering a season of great turmoil and testing. Last year (2023), I prophesied that we were embarking on a long, arduous journey, a journey filled with challenges that extend far beyond even sickness and disease. This is a tremendous spiritual battle. America, and indeed all of us, owe an outstanding debt in the spiritual realm, a debt that can only be paid through fervent intercession and faith in the power of God's redemption. But do not lose heart, for it is in times like these that we must rise up and take our place as intercessors before the throne of grace. There are things I have seen, I have shared some of them, while others have been kept, but now, more than ever, we must maintain our focus and determination because the strategies of the enemy are manifold, and the weapons forged by human hands have indeed contributed to the difficulties we face. But hear me well, child of God, no matter what visions of trouble I have seen, no matter what dire prophecies have been revealed to me, I stand firm in my conviction that our God, the Almighty, the All-Powerful, the Ever-Present One will protect you!*

Let's get back to the scripters.

Becoming An 'Empowerer'

In Genesis 12:1-3, You should realize that God's words to Abraham were not mere words, they were a divine covenant and a blueprint for blessings that extend to us today. The Lord said, *"I will bless you and make your name great. You will be a blessing to many."* This is the very essence of the blessing we are talking about. It is not just about personal prosperity or individual success. No, the true nature of God's blessing is far more expansive and more profound. It is about becoming a conduit of divine favor and a channel through which God's goodness can flow to the world around you.

Among the many definitions of blessing that I have shared over the years, I want us to focus on this fundamental truth that *"the blessing"* at its core is the *"empowerment"* of God and His divine license granted to us as well as His supernatural help bestowed upon us, that transforms us into what I call *"generational empowerers".* Write that term down, for it encapsulates the very essence of what it means to be truly blessed by God. When you fully understand the definition of *"the blessing"* and learn to apply it effectively in your life, you become more than just a recipient of God's favor, you become an agent of transformation and a catalyst for blessing in the lives of countless others.

Just take some moment to consider the magnitude of what God promised Abraham again God was practically saying *"I will bless you in such a way that your life will cause everyone in the world to be blessed."* This is not a hyperbole; it is a divine reality that God intends for each one of us. There is a dimension of blessing that extends beyond our immediate circumstances, beyond our families, and beyond our local communities. It is a blessing that has the potential to impact nations, to influence generations, to shape the course of history itself. This, my friend, is the true nature of God's blessing, it is not just for your benefit, but for the benefit of all humanity by making you an *"empowerer".*

Remember, the blessing is God's empowerment, His license, and His help, this means He is empowering you to achieve what would be impossible in your own strength, He is licensing you to operate with divine authority in every sphere of influence and He is helping you to overcome obstacles that would otherwise be insurmountable. But here's the critical part that you must never overlook, if you do not submit to His help, if you do not position yourself in line with His purposes, you risk living on the reverse side of the blessing. Yes, the blessing of God can indeed make a person rich and add no sorrow with it. But a person who lacks understanding of how to apply and manage God's blessing will quickly become arrogant, foolish, and proud. The very same blessing that is meant to bring joy, abundance, and positive impact will lead to destruction if it is misused or misunderstood.

This is why we sometimes witness the tragic spectacle of individuals who have been blessed by God, but who, due to their lack of understanding, end up causing sorrow and turmoil wherever they go. Instead of being channels of life and blessing, they inadvertently become agents of destruction using wealth, power, and influence to even destroy others. But I declare over you today, with all the authority vested in me as a servant of the Most High God, by reason of the blessing of God upon your life, wherever you go, good things will grow! Your presence will bring healing to the sick, hope to the despairing, and abundance to the impoverished. I decree that the blessing of God upon your life will cause barren situations to become fruitful, dead dreams to spring back to life, and impossible circumstances to bow IN THE MIGHTY NAME OF JESUS!

Take some more moments for deep introspection today and re-evaluate yourself, in line with all that we have discussed in this chapter. Are you truly walking in the fullness of God's blessing? Are you allowing yourself to be empowered, licensed, and helped by the Almighty? Are you becoming a generational empowerer, a conduit of blessing to the world around you? If not, why not? What patterns of thinking or behavior might be hindering the full manifestation of God's blessing in your life? Do not trivialize these questions because through them the Holy Spirit will open your mind and enlighten you in the mighty name of Jesus.

CHAPTER TWO

PRIORITIZING GOD - THE PATH TO THE BLESSING

❖ ❖ ❖

"No matter how powerful you are, without spiritual backing, victories can be short-lived. Stay humble before God, and let His divine favor sustain you."

❖ ❖ ❖

How Spiritual Backing Sustains Success

In the book of Chronicles, the bible gives us the remarkable story of a young boy named Uzziah, this was indeed a young boy whose life shows us the power of divine favor and spiritual guidance. At the tender age of 16 he ascended to the throne of Judah, and the blessings that flowed upon him were nothing short of extraordinary. He was truly and incredibly powerful and achieved tremendous success as well as accomplished numerous good deeds. His fame even spread far and wide, and he was feared throughout the world. But what was the secret behind this young king's astounding success? What propelled him to such heights of glory and renown?

The answer, child of God, lies in a simple, but yet profound truth of His spiritual mentorship. You see, Uzziah had a pastor, a man of God named Zechariah, who guided him in the ways of the Lord. The Bible says in 2 Chronicles 26:5 As long as Uzziah submitted himself to the counsel of his pastor Zachariah, he prospered. In other words, everything he set his hand to flourished, every endeavor bore fruit, and every step he took was a step forward. Indeed, the very heavens conspired to make his path smooth and his burdens light. For 52 long years, Uzziah sat upon the throne of Jerusalem, ruling with wisdom and might. The Bible tells us he was a loyal seeker of God, not just a seeker, but a loyal seeker. This was not a half-hearted pursuit or lukewarm devotion. No, Uzziah sought after God with all his heart, all his soul, and all his might. He sought God in the way God desired to be sought, with reverence, humility, and faith.

Now, let's consider the partnership that existed between the king and the priest, it was this divine partnership, this holy alliance, that allowed the office of King Uzziah to keep winning because he submitted to the office of Zachariah the priest. You see, no matter how smart or strong a king might be, his victories will be short-lived if he lacks the backing of a spiritual priest. He might win a battle here or there, but without that spiritual covering, disaster will surely come knocking at his door sooner or later. This is a revelation of why so many people seem not to be making headway in their lives; they are not progressing, they are not advancing, and they are not enjoying *"the blessings"* all because they do not have a priest over their life. Some others have, but they do not highly esteem the priest and so they still lack the spiritual backing that is supposed to come from that office to them.

The Moses' Example

Let's look at the example of Moses, another great leader of Israel, in Exodus 17. In the book of Exodus, when they were at war, Moses stood at the top of the mountain with his hands raised high, and as long as those hands remained lifted, Joshua and his warriors down in the valley kept on winning in the fight. What a sight that must have been! The power of intercessory prayer was made manifest before their very eyes! This is truly a clear picture of the critical role that spiritual support plays in our victories in life and in manifesting the blessings of God in our lives. Exodus 17:11 puts it this way

> *"And it came to pass, when Moses held up his hand, that Israel prevailed: and when he let down his hand, Amalek prevailed." (Exodus 17:11)*

I decree that you will win in any battle you are currently fighting in the name of Jesus!

But what happened when Moses' strength began to fail? When his arms grew weary and began to drop? The Bible tells us that the tides of the battle turned, and Israel began to lose ground. Those who stood with Moses on that mountaintop could see the cause of this sudden reversal of fortune. They understood the spiritual dynamics at play. Yet, they couldn't simply grab the rod from Moses' hand and start speaking in tongues, expecting everything to work out. That's not how the spiritual realm operates, my friends. You can't just pick up the mantle of authority and expect everything to fall into place without proper alignment, proper empowerment, and proper help. The spiritual realm demands respect for order and authority. It requires a heart that is properly attuned to the will of God and hands that are consecrated for His service. This is a crucial lesson for all of us who desire to walk in God's blessings and favor. And in their time only Moses possessed these qualities so no matter how tired he got, they had to look for a way to ensure that his hands remained up

So, what did they do? They brought a stone for Moses to sit upon, and Aaron and Hur stood on either side of him, holding up his hands until the sun went down. And because of this act of support and unity, Joshua was able to defeat Amalek and their army. The Bible says it this way

> *But Moses' hands were heavy; and they took a stone, and put it under him, and he sat thereon; and Aaron and Hur stayed up his hands, the one on the one side, and the other on the other side; and his hands were steady until the going down of the sun." (Exodus 17:12)*

What a powerful lesson this is, you must never neglect or esteem lowly the Pastor or Prophet of God over your life, and just in case you do not have one, you better get one and submit loyally today. Do you realize that no matter how powerful Joshua may have been, he would have obviously failed on the battlefield and maybe even lost his life if Moses decided to leave the mountain? Just as Uzziah had the backing of Zachariah, Joshua had the Backing of Moses, and David also had the backing of Samuel, so take a look at your own life, who is your spiritual backing? Who is bringing you support from the spirit realm? If you cannot get this straight, you probably should forget about enjoying the blessings of God in full measure.

I lift my hands to the throne of grace on your behalf today, and I decree that you will continue to win from this day! Wherever you have been losing, begin to win! Wherever you have already been winning, you will win even better! Wherever you go, good things will grow in the name of Jesus! The evil in your environment will bow before you and the one seeking to destroy you will be cast down in the name of Jesus!

But remember, with great blessing comes great responsibility. As we will see in Uzziah's story, it is not enough to start well; you must always strive to finish well, too. You must guard your hearts against pride and never forget the source of our blessings.

Blessings And Pride

Uzziah's Rise, Fall, And The Danger of Forgetting God

So back to Chronicles, Uzziah was a loyal seeker of God, and as long as he continually sought after God, he prospered.

Uzziah was well-trained by his pastor, Zechariah, to serve God in the way God wanted. To be well-trained means to learn not just to serve, but to serve in obedience to how God desires, not according to your own preferences. This is a crucial distinction that many of us miss in our walk with God. We often want to serve God on our own terms in ways that are comfortable or convenient for us. But accurate service, the kind that brings God's blessings, requires us to align our will with His, even when it is challenging or uncomfortable.

This is very important because many people get lost chasing after things that aren't in line with God's will for them. These are the kinds who we can say are chasing shadows, which will never result in catching substance, it is an endless pursuit that will leave you empty-handed. Have you ever experienced this in your life, chasing after worldly success, material possessions, and even human approval, only to find that these things do not bring the fulfillment and satisfaction you sought? It is like trying to grasp at smoke, the more you reach for it, the more it will elude you.

In 2 Chronicles 26:15, the bible tells us that God marvelously helped Uzziah and became well-known for his accomplishments. I want you to declare *"I will be well-known for the product of God's blessing upon my life." Amen!*

This is not about seeking fame for its own sake, but about allowing God's blessings in our lives to become a testament to His goodness and power so that men will see and give Him glory. When God empowers, licenses, and assists you, things naturally go your way. From today, I declare that things will go your way in Jesus' name! Why? Because God knows He can trust you to use His power and blessing for His purpose, not against Him. This is a critical point, God's blessings are not for our own selfish gain alone, but for the advancement of His kingdom and the benefit of others.

Take Caution

But here's the challenge: once God empowers and licenses you, you must continue to rely on His help. If you do not meet the conditions to sustain His help, things can go wrong. This is where many, who once were blessed, falter, they soon become the very downfall of their own prophetic destinies. This is why I said earlier that it is not enough to start well, we must finish well too. Know that the journey of faith is a marathon and not a sprint, and you must remain dependent on God every step of the way.

Look at what happened to Uzziah. In 2 Chronicles 26:16 (The Message Translation); it says:

"But then the strength and success went to his head."

This means He became proud, and he fell hard. Not just a slight stumble, but a fall so big it is what we call, in African terms, "yakata". In other words, it was a complete collapse! Wow, what a cautionary reminder of the dangers of pride and self-reliance. No matter how blessed or prosperous you become, you must never forget the source of your blessings. I can assure you that you will succeed in the name of Jesus, but as you rise and grow, remember to keep your heart humble and your eyes fixed on God. Do not let success go to your head like it did with Uzziah.

Let us see it in the scriptures

2 Chronicles 26:16 -21

[16] But after Uzziah became powerful, his pride led to his downfall. He was unfaithful to the Lord his God and entered the temple of the Lord to burn incense on the altar of incense. [17] Azariah the priest with eighty other courageous priests of the Lord followed him in. [18] They confronted King Uzziah and said, "It is not right for you, Uzziah, to burn incense to the Lord. That is for the priests, the descendants of Aaron, who have been consecrated to burn incense. Leave the sanctuary, for you have been unfaithful; and you will not be honored by the Lord God." [19] Uzziah, who had a censer in his hand ready to burn incense, became angry. While he was raging at the priests in their presence before the incense altar in the Lord's temple, leprosy broke out on his forehead. [20] When Azariah the chief priest and all the other priests looked at him, they saw that he had leprosy on his forehead, so they hurried him out. Indeed, he was eager to leave because the Lord had afflicted him. [21] King Uzziah had leprosy until the day he died. He lived in a separate house—leprous and banned from the temple of the Lord. Jotham his son had charge of the palace and governed the people of the land.

A primary way to guide against this kind of fall is to always have in mind the higher purposes for which God blesses us.

So, why does God bless us? I have said it before and I will keep saying it again and again *"God blesses us to empower us for the advancement of His Kingdom and for the betterment of the world. Every gift, opportunity, and resource He provides is meant to bring glory to Him and to further His purposes"* I am not saying you shouldn't enjoy and have fun as the blessings comes, of course you will, but if you lose sight of those higher purposes then there is a tendency that you may fall into the trap of the product of the blessing becoming the object of your worship instead of God who is the giver of the blessing. This is when most people begin to lose the help that sustains them because, like Uzziah, they are becoming carried away with achievements and accomplishments.

I will say it again in another way, *"when the blessing which was meant to be a tool for serving God, turns into the idol you pursue, you will lose His help"* But you won't only lose the help of God, you will lose his favor, his protection, his guidance and you will become porous for the devil to attack and you may eventually lose your life. This is the peril of Uzziah. Instead of remaining humble and reliant on God, he became arrogant and proud, forgetting that it was God who had empowered him in the first place.

Let this be a lesson to you that you must never allow the blessing to become your god; you must stay humble, obedient, and reliant on God all the days of your life, for that is the key to sustaining the blessings He has poured out upon you. It is so easy to fall into this trap, is not it? We focus on the blessings, wealth, success, and recognition rather than on the One who blessed us. We begin to think that we have achieved these things by our strength or intelligence, forgetting that every perfect gift comes from above. Look at the words of Deuteronomy 8:17-18,

> *"And thou say in thine heart, My power and the might of mine hand hath gotten me this wealth. But thou shalt remember the LORD thy God: for it is he that giveth thee power to get wealth, that he may establish his covenant which he sware unto thy fathers, as it is this day."*

This scripture calls attention again to the fact that all our success and wealth ultimately come from God, and they are given to us for a purpose: to establish His covenant and further His kingdom.

You must be vigilant against the creeping influence of pride in your lives because pride is subtle, and it can even disguise itself as self-confidence or self-reliance, but true confidence comes from knowing who we are in Christ and relying on His strength, not our own (James 4:6)

So how do we guard against pride and maintain a humble, God-dependent attitude even amid success and blessing? Here are a few practical steps:

- You must daily acknowledge God as the source of your blessings and start each day by thanking Him for His goodness and recognizing that everything you have comes from Him.
- You should regularly seek God's guidance, even in areas where you feel competent, because this will help you maintain an attitude of dependence on Him.
- Be very sincere in your local church and submit to spiritual authority; this will help you counteract the tendency towards self-sufficiency, which often comes with success.

Do not forget that the goal is not to reject or diminish the blessings God gives us but to keep them in proper perspective, knowing fully well that we are stewards and not owners of these blessings. So, our role is to manage and multiply them for God's glory, not to hoard them for our own selfishness. I pray that you will truly learn from the life of Isaiah, first of all, that you must honor the spiritual authority God has placed over your life, and secondly, that you will never allow the blessings of God to lead you into corruption in any way.

How To Understand Your True Idols And Priorities

One key point here you must never forget is that when the blessings of God or any other thing begins to take God's place in your heart, it also begins to take precedence over God in your priorities and decisions. You will find yourself chasing it more passionately than you chase after God's will. So many people even fall into this pit without knowing until it is too late. Sometimes, this shift in priorities can disguise itself as a necessary dedication to work or other responsibilities. Still, if you are not careful, these pursuits will become idols that steal your devotion from God, blind your eyes to your relationship with Him, lead you to a place where you trust your effort more than God, and eventually, you will become lifted in yourself and fully ready for the enemy to strike you down.

But let us examine some key areas that will help us discern if you have fallen or are falling into this trap:

- **Prioritization:**
  When you can stay up all night for a business deal, drinking coffee to remain alert and focused, but you can't muster the same energy or sacrifice when God calls you to fast and pray, it shows where your devotion lies. If worldly pursuits like business or financial success make you work harder than your spiritual growth or obedience to God, that pursuit has become an object of worship. This misalignment of priorities clearly indicates that something has taken God's place in your heart. The Bible warns us about this in Matthew 6:24,
  "No man can serve two masters: for either he will hate the one, and love the other, or else he will hold to the one, and despise the other. Ye cannot serve God and mammon."
  You must constantly examine your hearts and actions to ensure that God remains your top priority, not just in word, but indeed.
- **Effort:**
  When you can spend more energy, resources, and time to see that anything works, maybe your relationship, your business, even spending effort to create a good, fun time, but give up easily when it comes to spiritual things, then it means your heart has shifted or is gradually shifting; also If you see that in your life the Lord's desires are becoming secondary when they should be primary, then it reveals that *"the object"* or *"that thing"* which your effort if entirely directed at may have become your

idol. See, as human beings, our efforts reflect the true desires of our hearts, and if you find yourself pouring more energy into your worldly pursuits than into your relationship with God, then you need to sit down and call yourself to order by setting your heart right again.

- **Sacrifice:**

When you see that you are willing to sacrifice time, energy, resources, comfort, and even more for the sake of anything or anyone but struggle to sacrifice for God, there is a challenge. When you are unwilling to make the same sacrifices for your relationship with God that you will make for the sake of money, for example, it shows you are putting more importance on earthly rewards than on spiritual growth; this disparity in your willingness to sacrifice reveals the true priorities of your hearts.

- **Excuses:**

If you give excuses to justify something and keep finding reasons why issues concerning your spiritual life should be pushed back, then there is a challenge; it means God is no longer at the top of your list. You might even rationalize it by saying, *"I need to work; I have responsibilities, and I have bills to pay,"* but when God calls you to pray or fast, you come up with excuses. If you are willing to inconvenience yourself for the sake of paying bills but not for spiritual matters, do you not see that this is a clear indication that the blessing (work, wealth, status) is becoming more critical than the Blesser (God) to you? Look at what the book of Luke 14:18-20 says, *"And they all with one consent began to make an excuse. The first said unto him, I had bought a piece of ground, and I must go and see it: I pray thee have me excused. And another said, I have bought five yoke of oxen, and I go to prove them: I pray thee have me excused. And another said, I have married a wife, so I cannot come."* Though these excuses seemed valid, they only revealed the true priorities of those invited. Similarly, when we make excuses to avoid spiritual disciplines or service to God while accommodating worldly pursuits, we are revealing that our hearts are not fully devoted to God.

From all these, I believe you can now see that the worship of the product of the blessing happens when we become more focused on the blessings God gives (like money, success, influence, etc.) than on God Himself. This is when we forget that He is the source, and instead, we shift our focus to maintaining or expanding those blessings, even at the cost of our relationship with Him. Prophet Hosea spoke about thin in Hosea 13:6,

> "According to their pasture, so were they filled; they were filled, and their heart was exalted; therefore have they forgotten me."

This verse shows how prosperity can lead to pride and forgetfulness of God if we're not careful to maintain our dependence on Him.

Child of God, the Lord wants us to follow His guidance and keep our eyes on Him, especially in challenging times. When difficult situations arise, the only way to stand firm is by keeping God first and not allowing the things of this world to distract you. I am repeating this from the bottom of my heart, if you become too focused on your career, success, or other pursuits, you risk losing spiritual focus and falling into pride, arrogance, and ultimately, failure. Psalm 121:1-2 says

> "I will lift mine eyes unto the hills, from whence cometh my help. My help cometh from the LORD, which made heaven and earth."

This should be your constant attitude of always looking to God.

CHAPTER THREE

SPIRITUAL DISCIPLINES FOR WALKING IN THE BLESSINGS

◆ ◆ ◆

"The discipline of giving, even when difficult, shapes your spirit for greater blessings. It is not the amount; it is the heart behind the act."

◆ ◆ ◆

The Training Of Faith Through Financial Struggles

L et me tell you something, and you might not like hearing it, but it is the truth: God asks for the first fruits to teach us humility; why does He demand tithes? It is to maintain a constant, unbreakable connection between us and Him. Have you noticed that if you are sitting down with everything you need and start thinking about the first fruit offering, you suddenly will find yourself in a place where you feel like you have nothing left?

Of course, some people are clever and may plan, thinking, *"I will set aside this money so that when it is time for the first fruits, I can give it without breaking a sweat, and then I will know exactly how to move forward."* And sure, that's a smart way to go about it. But not everybody has enough resources to act this way, and now you are thinking, worried, and scared that if you give your first fruit, you will have to struggle through life for a season; that's precisely where God wants you to be.

It may even seem that He is oblivious that you are behind in your bills, but what? That's the key right there. Being behind is meant to put you in a place where you have no choice but to humble yourself and say, *"Oh, my Father, I trust You completely."* When you start moving forward again, you won't be stuck in the realm of struggle anymore. You will enter a new dimension were giving the first fruits of ten million dollars won't cost you a wink of sleep, and you won't feel behind on anything. Why? Because the Lord has trained you, and he has now blessed you. Sometimes, it looks like God is hard on you because He is training you, molding you, and shaping you into someone who can handle abundance without being self-centered or letting it go to your head.

Has it ever occurred to you that God could easily snap His fingers and shower you with all the money in the world overnight? But then again, if you are still walking around with an arrogant spirit and if you have not been trained to live faithfully when times are tough, that wealth will only destroy you; it will not make you a better person; instead, it may bring out the worst in you because you have not been trained. So instead of just loading you with all the money, God always supplies your needs, and does it in a way that tests your faith, demanding you keep trusting Him every day and every time. Maybe you need one hundred dollars, but God only gave you five. Do you know what He is doing? He's watching you like a hawk and observing what you will do with those five dollars.

You may think, *"Well, Lord, thank You for the five dollars! I will take my tithe - fifty cents."* Now, I know what you are probably thinking.

Fifty cents? That's too small for a tithe! God is not in heaven, hungry for your loose change. My spiritual grandfather used to say, and I will never forget this, *"God does not need your wretched dollars for His existence."* When you look at the book of Malachi, that's exactly what the Bible's saying. God is calling out His people, saying, *"You are bringing me these lame offerings. Do you honestly think I need your pathetic sacrifices?"* Read Malachi 1:6-8

> *"Will a man rob God? Yet ye have robbed me. But ye say, wherein have we robbed thee? In tithes and offerings." (Malachi 3:8)*

So, what's the real goal here? It is all about the principle and the heart behind the giving. If, for example, I'm blessed with twenty dollars, and I take out my two dollars for the levy, it might seem insignificant; after all, It is only two dollars. But I tell you the truth, it is a training ground, you may look down on it and despise it, but when you do that, you are sending the wrong kind of intelligence to your altar. And when it is time for God to show up in your life, your altar will send back the feedback saying, *"Nope, this one does not value the principle; therefore, He is not ready for the big blessings."*

You may be sitting down there, waiting for the day you become a millionaire, and then you will start giving, paying your tithe, and more... But God does not work like that, so he He's saying, *"No way! Before I gave Abraham Isaac, I asked for his foreskin. Before I gave him the promise, I asked for his Isaac."* That's the process, and you, too, must master the art of giving if you are going to enjoy some dimensions of His blessings; only through mastering this financial training will you qualify for some level of financial blessings.

The Necessity Of Faithfulness

In Genesis 17:1 The Bible says

> *"And when Abram was ninety years old and nine, the Lord appeared to Abram, and said unto him, I am the Almighty God; walk before me, and be thou perfect."*

The core demand here from God to Abraham in this place is a demand for faithfulness, not necessarily going through life and making sure he is 100% perfect in character. None of us can live that way, and that's why we will always need the mercy and grace of God. When you can learn to show yourself faithful in the little things, God says, *"Alright, now I can trust you with more. I will make you a ruler over many things."*

Child of God, if you suddenly begin to notice that God is not helping you the way He used to, then it is time to do a heart check, yes, it is time to check your heart! Do you want to know a foolproof way to measure the condition of your heart? Look at your commitment to God, especially financial commitment and giving God your time; these two things will reveal whether your heart is on fire for Him, cold as ice, or just putting on a show for everyone else. This is a reason none of us can afford to be far from God, you must walk closely with Him so that He will always be able to show you what you are missing as you journey with Him. And any moment the Lord shows you anything you must be quick to respond in obedience, do not lag, and ensure you do not disobey. That's when He really takes notice; He loves a quick and heartfelt response.

Giving Opens You Up To Receive

By now, you should have known that God is not poor and hungry and is not looking for your money to survive. I said this to let you know that your giving and your passing on God's financial training are ultimately for your good. Yes, it benefits you more than anyone else because it opens you up to more blessings.

When you consistently give, even when it hurts and even when you do not see immediate results, you are building spiritual muscle, and you are proving to God that you can be trusted with more. It is like working out; the more you exercise your faith through giving, the stronger it becomes for receiving. Luke 6:38 says,

> *"Give, and it shall be given unto you; good measure, pressed down, shaken together, and running over, shall men give into your bosom. With the same measure that ye mete withal, it shall be measured to you again."*

Although material blessings are great and part of this scripture, I also want you to know that this verse is not limited to material blessings. It is about an overflow in every area of your life, an overflow that's only possible when you pass the training of becoming a consistent giver. Through giving, you are showing God that you understand His economy, that you know everything comes from Him, and that you are willing to be a channel of His blessings, not just a reservoir.

Another beautiful thing about giving is that it may be difficult when you initially start giving. Still, as you keep doing it, the Lord keeps releasing His grace upon you, and in your faithfulness towards giving, you will notice that the struggle to provide begins to reduce, the anxiety over giving will begin to diminish, and the level of joy and fulfillment you experience when you give will also start to multiply thereby making a lot easier to give which also means making it a lot easier to receive from God.

But remember, it is not just about the amount, it is about the heart; God is not impressed by big numbers, instead He is moved by immense faith, trust, and a heart that genuinely gives because you want to see His kingdom go far or because you want to see the needy happy. If you only keep giving so that you will keep getting, then please, you are not a giver. You are just a businessman. Yes, I agree that you may experience some levels of increase that way, but do not call yourself a giver; you are just a businessman following a kingdom principle. So I want to encourage you right now, whether you are at the level of giving fifty cents or fifty thousand dollars, give it with a heart full of love, commitment, and gratitude to the Lord, even when you are giving to the needy, the orphanage, the helpless, always say to yourself, "I am doing it unto the Lord" and then Give it knowing that you are participating in God's great plan of redemption and provision.

As you pass this training of giving, you will find yourself stepping into a new level of spiritual maturity; you will become a trustworthy steward of God's resources, someone He can use to bless others on a grand scale. And is not that what it is all about? Becoming a conduit of God's love and provision to a world in desperate need?

Please do not despise the days of small beginnings. Embrace the training, welcome the tests, and as long as you prove faithful in little, I assure you that you will experience God's blessings in glorious ways and that He will continually entrust you with much. And before you know it, you will be walking in abundance and blessing you never thought possible, all because you learned the sacred art of giving.

Hearing As A Gate To Receiving More Blessings

Let me share something powerful that will change how you walk with God. We had this situation recently, a fire breakout that could have been disastrous, and I thank God for what happened, you see I did not share it in church, but I opened up to some of our beloved ones about it. But then as I was reflecting on this incident on a particular day, God spoke to me, and when God speaks, you better listen. He said, *"Have I been good to you?"* I said, *"Yes Sir,"*

He said it again, about three to five times, then I began to wonder, *"Am I missing something?"* He then said to me *"Do you know that the enemy had planned for your vehicle to explode on the road"* Can you imagine how catastrophic that would have been? So, I said *"Yes sir, I even shared with some people"* So he said, *"Good, but you have not celebrated with me by giving thanks in church."* Now, that caught me off guard. I asked, *"Sir, what do you mean?"* His response was clear as day, He said *"The church has not taken the time to dance about this testimony."* It hit me hard, indeed we had acknowledged the miracle, sure, but we had not truly celebrated it. We had not allowed the joy of God's protection to overwhelm us and lead us to worship praise, thanksgiving, and dancing. Immediately, we planned the Thanksgiving serving in church, and it was a glorious time of joy in God's presence, appreciating Him.

Now, you might wonder, *"How did you hear God so clearly?"* Well, it is because there's nothing He tells me to do that I won't follow through on. It is a relationship built on trust and obedience. How did I get to this point? By being humble in the little things, every single little thing. If you cannot be humble and quick in obeying His voice, then I assure you that you will struggle to continually hear Him.

Think about it, the last time he gave you an instruction did you obey? When he said wake up and pray did you? When he said help that needy brother did you, when he said make sure you do not miss church did you? If you cannot follow the little and basic instructions, then please stop expecting to hear God clearer and better and quit expecting Him to give you greater instructions. James 1:22 gives us a caution that we must not only hear but must also be willing to do and this is how the blessings will come.

> Read it for yourself *"But be ye doers of the word, and not hearers only, deceiving your own selves." (James 1:22)*

It is my greatest desire that you will come to understand the necessity of obedience when God speaks as well as realize that without the guidance of His voice you will never walk in high realms of blessings. If the last time God spoke to you was four years ago, then you should know that He is still waiting for you to act on what He said!

The Path To Receiving More

The reason I shared my story about the fire incident and God's demand that we praise Him in church was to show you that in my life I always want to respond to God as fast as possible when he speaks. Do you realize that as long as we are in this world we will always need some form of direction? In your finances you need direction, in running your business you need direction, in running your home you need direction. One of the greatest needs of we human beings is *"direction"* Who do I ask to help me? How do I get a good Job? How do I receive my healing? Who is the right spouse to marry? What course should I study in school? How do I make my spouse value me better? We can keep the list going on, and on, and on. But at the end of the day, all these are simply questions on *"direction"*, they are questions of what to do, when to do, and how to do things.

When this revelation finally dawns on you, you will begin to realize why you cannot joke with the issue of being able to hear and obey the voice of God. Listening to God is the surest way to open the door to more of His blessings, and when you tune your ear to God's voice, I mean when you truly make it a priority to hear Him and respond promptly, you are positioning yourself for an overflow of blessings, because you will also be positioning yourself to have all your questions, especially the ones on direction to be answered by the God who truly knows everything and can guide you in a way that no man and no counselor will ever be able to guide you. Do not forget, it is not just about hearing; it is about hearing and doing!

When God speaks and you act, you are demonstrating faith, and faith is the currency of heaven.

> *"But without faith, it is impossible to please him: for he that cometh to God must believe that he is, and that he is a rewarder of them that diligently seek him." (Hebrews 11:6).*

By the time you are able to cultivate a lifestyle of listening and obeying, you are building a track record with God, you are showing Him that you can be trusted with more instructions and you are also saying you are ready for higher dimensions of the blessings and glory in your life. It is like you are saying, *"Lord, I'm ready for whatever You have for me. I'm listening, and I'm willing to act on what I hear."* God loves this kind of attitude.

If you truly can commit yourself to continually listen and respond to God's voice in this way, then I assure you that you will find yourself walking in a level of wisdom and discernment that goes beyond human understanding. You will make decisions that might not make sense to the world but align perfectly with God's plan for your life, and as you walk in this divine wisdom, doors will open that you never even knew existed.

But here's the thing, it is not always going to be easy when obedience is demanded by God because sometimes, His voice will lead you to do things that seem counterintuitive to the human mind, He will tell you to give when you feel like you need to get more from people, He will direct you to step out in faith when everything in you wants to play it safe, but do you know what? Let me assure you, obedience to God's voice always leads to great blessing, it may not come in the package you expect, but it will come, and it will be far better than anything you could have orchestrated on your own.

So, how do you cultivate this ability to hear God's voice? It starts with spending time in His presence. You have to create space in your life for God to speak and this means carving out time for prayer, for studying His Word, for quiet reflection; and it also means turning down the noise of the world and tuning in to the frequency of heaven.

And when you hear His voice, do not hesitate, act on it even if it is just a small prompting. When you do this consistently, you will discover that His voice keeps becoming louder and clearer; and your ability to discern His leading will become sharper also, thereby moving you from the level of hearing God occasionally to living in constant communion with Him.

This, my friends, is the pathway to receiving more from God. It is not about asking for more blessings; it is about positioning yourself to be a better steward of what He has already given so that more can naturally flow into your life and even through your life. Do not forget that God is not looking for perfect people, He is just looking for willing hearts and for those who are ready to say *"yes"* to Him, even when it is difficult. He's looking for those who will trust Him enough to step out onto the water when He calls. And as you become that person, as you cultivate that kind of relationship with Him, you will find yourself walking in Higher dimensions of the blessing.

An Easy Guide To Effectively Hearing The Voice Of God

Now before we get into it, this is not some mystical, out-of-reach experience reserved for the super-spiritual people. Hearing God's voice is the birthright of every believer, and I am going to show you how to step into this divine dialogue with confidence and clarity.

Step 1: Cultivate A Heart Of Expectancy And

Stillness

The first step in hearing God's voice is that you must cultivate a heart that expects to hear Him Speak. If you go about thinking He is too high and mighty and will never speak to you, this makes it a whole lot difficult to hear because your faith and trust that He loves and cares about you is already shattered. Meanwhile, faith is always the foundation of doing anything with God. Too many times, believers go through life with their spiritual ears plugged by living a life where they are never anticipating that the Lord will stoop down to speak to them. But you must know this now, He is always saying, the question is, are you always listening? Now, you cultivate this expectancy, you will need to create moments of stillness in your life. In today's fast-moving world, with all its noise and distractions, you must intentionally carve out time to be still before God. This comprises of physical quietness, stilling your mind, calming your emotions, and focusing your spirit on God. This is how to create an atmosphere where His voice will be able to cut through the clutter of your daily life.

"Be still, and know that I am God: I will be exalted among the heathen, I will be exalted in the earth." (Psalm 46:10)

This is not a suggestion; it is a command with a promise. When you finally know how to become still, I mean truly still in your heart, you will come to know God in a deeper way. And in that knowing, you will become more attuned to His voice. So, start your day with moments of stillness, before you check your phone, before you turn on the TV, before you engage with the world, engage with God. Just sit in His presence, quiet your heart, and expect Him to speak.

Step 2: Keep Yourself In The Word Of God

In hearing God's voice, you must also know this and never forget it. God will never speak to you in a way that contradicts His written Word because The Bible is the foundation for hearing God's voice; it is like the tuning fork that helps you recognize the pitch of His voice in your spirit. Psalm 119:105 captures it beautifully by saying,

> *"Thy word is a lamp unto my feet and a light unto my path.".*

When you keep yourself in the scriptures, you familiarize yourself with God's language, character, and communication methods. The more you know the Word, the easier it will become to discern His voice in your daily life. I am not just saying you should do a casual reading of the Bible; it is not enough to read the Bible casually; you have to study it, meditate on it, and let it seep into the very fibers of your being.

Make it a habit not just to read, but to actively engage with the Word. Ask questions as you read. Ponder the meanings. Apply it to your life. As you do this consistently, you'll find that verses will pop into your mind at just the right moment, giving you guidance, comfort, or direction. That's God speaking to you through His Word!

Step 3: Practice Obedience In The Small Things

I talked about obedience earlier, but I will take time to emphasize it again. Know *this "Your ability to hear God's voice is directly related to your willingness to obey what He has already told you".* Think about this for a moment, if you are ignoring the clear instructions in His Word, why would He give you a more specific direction? John 14:15 says, *"If ye love me, keep my commandments."* You need to know that Obedience is not just about following rules; it is about aligning your life with God's will, and it is about saying *"yes"* to God even when it is inconvenient or challenging. When you practice obedience in the small things, in how you treat others, in your integrity at work, and in your faithfulness with your resources, you are creating a pathway for God's voice to flow more freely in your life. So, I will advise you to start paying attention to those small promptings in your spirit. Maybe it is an urge to call someone, to pray for a situation, or to give to a specific need, do not just brush these off. Act on them. As you prove faithful in these little things, God will entrust you with greater insights and directions.

Step 4: Submit To People Who Are Deep In Hearing God

Now, let's be clear here, Hearing God's voice is not something you just jump into, especially when you have to make life-changing decisions. Just one wrong decision and you may end up destroying yourself in a very terrible way. You need the body of Christ to help you discern and confirm what you are hearing. That's why being part of a strong, Bible-believing church is very important. By being in a good church, it is easier to relate with mature believers and even the Shepherd of God over your life to ensure that what you are hearing is correct. The bible says

> "Where no counsel is, the people fall: but in the multitude of counsellors there is safety." (Proverbs 11:14)

Do not ever neglect the place of surrounding yourself with mature believers who can give you godly counsel. When you think you've heard from God, especially regarding major decisions, run it by your spiritual mentors and let them pray with you, offer their insights, and help you test what you are hearing against Scripture.

And speaking of testing, it is a very important part of developing discernment, 1 John 4:1 says

"Beloved, believe not every spirit, but try the spirits whether they are of God" (1 John 4:1).

Not every thought or impression that pops into your head is from God, even the devil sometimes pretends to be an angel of light so you must forever be careful.

Here are some questions to ask when you think you have heard from God:

- Does it align with Scripture?
- Does it promote love for God and others?
- Does it lead to freedom or bondage?
- Does it bring peace or anxiety?
- Does it glorify God or elevate self?

As you consistently apply these tests, you will become more adept at distinguishing God's voice from your own thoughts or the enemy's deceptions.

I will also want you to know that hearing God's voice is a lifetime journey of growth and refinement so do not get discouraged if you do not always get it right, even the most seasoned prophets in the Bible sometimes misheard or misinterpreted God's voice. Imagine when Samuel almost anointed the wrong people seven times. God had to correct him and say, hey, young man I do not see the way men see. Is not that amazing? The key is to keep seeking, keep listening, and keep obeying. And do not ever lose hope because just as every father wants to talk to their child, so also does God always want to talk to you, even more than you want to hear from Him. He's not playing hide and seek, He's not trying to make it difficult, and He's a loving Father who delights in communicating with His children every day!

As you grow in this area, your entire life will take a dramatic turn, your decisions will be better and your destiny will be clearer. You will be able to walk with a level of confidence that comes from knowing you are in line with God's plan for your life, and that, my friend, is a major part of the abundant life Jesus came to give us.

CHAPTER FOUR

BLESSED TO BE A GENERATIONAL FORCE FOR GOD'S KINGDOM

◆ ◆ ◆

"God's intention is not just to bless you, but to make you a blessing to generations"

◆ ◆ ◆

Becoming A Generational Blessing

Understanding God's Beautiful Intention

One of the heart desires of God is that He does not just want to bless you, He wants to make you a generational blessing as well. When the Lord first said this to me, I asked Him what He meant by a generational blessing, and His answer was very profound. He told me that *"whoever desires to be a generational blessing must accept the responsibility of providing leadership at every level until they become global leaders"*. Now, do not rush, you should take your time to read that again. So, what does it mean to be a generational blessing? It means accepting the responsibility of providing leadership in every aspect of your life until you become a global force to be reckoned with. This has now gone far beyond the level of personal success or material wealth; it is about embracing a higher call that impacts live, families, nations, and generations to come.

In other words, the Lord is saying that He is not only blessing you just so you may have a car for example. Owning a car only requires hard work, but enjoying that car, and having peace of mind as you drive it, that requires His blessing. How about a bed, buying a good bed may cost you some money, but having peace in it, a restful life, and a sweet sleep, the kind that rejuvenates your soul, requires His blessing. Having a roof over your head may require your hard work and money, but creating a happy home filled with joy and peace, that's where His blessing comes in. You see, God's blessings go beyond the material world, they are meant to touch every aspect of our lives so as to bringing fulfillment, joy, purpose, and all that God intended from the very foundations of the world.

Proverbs 10:22 captures all this in an amazing way when it tells us that the blessings of the Lord, makes rich and adds no sorrow with it. When you start working with God by truly aligning yourself with His will and His ways, you will definitely experience this dimension every day of your life. He will ensure that you receive both the car and the divine protection that comes with it, His blessings will provide you with not just the house, but the home, a true place of refuge and joy. Not just the job, but the joy that makes your work fulfilling.

Has it ever occurred to you that there are people out there who have jobs but lack joy? That's why most people are usually angry on Mondays, they know that when Mondays come, they won't be happy at work, they keep going every day as though they are going to prison. They may go to work, but they lack satisfaction in what they do since their work feels like a burden rather than a calling. But God wants better for you, His intention and desire is to give you both the life and health to enjoy your life fully; to give you not just a job but a job that will fill your heart will joy and gladness.

God Has Called You To Be A Global Leader.

Remember I said the intention is not to bless you alone, the Lord also wants to give you *"power"*, His license and authorization to lead your generation, is not that wonderful? Being assisted by God is one of the most amazing things that can happen to you. When God assists you, nothing can resist you. Anything or anyone that stands in opposition to you will fall because God is fighting on your behalf. Isaiah 54:17 says

> *"No weapon that is formed against thee shall prosper; and every tongue that shall rise against thee in judgment thou shalt condemn. This is the heritage of the servants of the Lord, and their righteousness is of me, saith the Lord."*

This is a very powerful promise and an assurance that by aligning ourselves with the Lord we soon become unstoppable when it comes to making an impact and touching lives. This is the essence of being called to be a generational leader.

It is so you can be a blessing to everyone around you and so you can truly function as the light of the world as Jesus said in Matthew 5:14,

> *"Ye are the light of the world. A city that is set on an hill cannot be hid."*

I do not care how high you may think you are right now or how low you may think you are, what I am going to say right now is that *"At your level, you should start demonstrating leadership"*. If you have younger siblings, brothers, or sisters, you should show them how to lead. You can lead your siblings even if they are older than you. In fact, my siblings who are older than me still call me *"Daddy."* This is possible because I have chosen to be an ambassador of heaven and to function in my call as a generational leader. I show them how to be who God wants them to be and this kind of leadership is a leadership that transcends age, time, and position into eternity.

What Does It Take To Be A Generational Leader?

Think about it for a moment; what does it take to become a generational leader? Let us discuss four things that God desires for you to lead with if you want to be a generational leader:

- **God-inspired ideas**

If you truly want to be the kind of leader that will have a generational impact, then you cannot afford to lead with the method of *"trial and error".* You must be inspired of God; we can also call it divine revelation. You see, God wants you to be full of His inspired thoughts so that when you lead your world, you will be influencing it with His ideas and the first demand for this is plugging yourself deep into the Scriptures, seeking God's wisdom through prayer, and allowing the Holy Spirit to guide your decision and actions every day. The goal is to develop your mind in line with the scriptures and with the Holy Spirit so that you and God will always be on the same page whenever you are about to make choices or decisions.

- **Be cautious of influences:**

It is such a shame today that our world has to continually grapple with demonic concepts of worldliness every day. In light of this you must be careful of the people you allow into your inner cycle, people you call friends and people you associate with. No matter what happens do not allow people just jump into your life with stupid ideologies, just because they may be influential one way or the other. Their ideas can lead you to compromise your destiny as well as end up destroying yourself. I know the bible says you are to love everybody, but there is nowhere in scripture where we are told to associate with everybody, this means you can love people, however, you do not have to be close with them.

When you see a minister of God, for example, braiding his hair, and wearing earrings, nose rings, and other kinds of stuff. The question you need to ask yourself is *"What is he chasing"* or *"What is chasing him?"* What is he pursuing? Think about Lot; what do you think gave his daughters the effrontery to get their father drunk and sleep with him? It is probably because his daughters saw so much profanity while living in Sodom and Gomorrah. They were already influenced by their environment; this is why his daughters could violate him. Truly, there are things you must not seek to understand because sometimes; in attempting to comprehend such matters, you may become a victim. The Scripture warns us in Romans 16:19,

"For your obedience is come abroad unto all men. I am glad therefore on your behalf: but yet I would have you wise unto that which is good, and simple concerning evil."

This divine wisdom is an instruction for us to discern the influences we allow into our lives, focusing on what is good and pure rather than being entangled in worldly controversies. If you are not careful wrong movies, music, shows, friends, and colleagues will all derail you from the path of destiny only to your early grave just like the old and young prophet (1Kings 13:1-32)

· **Understanding your boundaries**

As you pursue your leadership in line with God's ordination and calling for your life, you must remain rooted in Christ. Do not compromise your values or allow the world's ideas to dictate your life. Do not cross the boundaries of Christian conduct, discipline, and lifestyle into becoming anything not of God. The moment you do that you will end up like Uzziah or probably like Saul and several other kings who crossed the line. Romans 12:2 says

"And be not conformed to this world: but be ye transformed by the renewing of your mind, that ye may prove what is that good, and acceptable, and perfect, will of God."

The Lord has called us to stand out, and not to conform to the world. So, if you truly want to be a global leader and a generational blessing, you must maintain the boundaries. Your life must be black or white; no grey areas are allowed!

- **Stay Rooted in the Lord:**

This is the foundation upon which all aspects of global leadership and being a generational blessing are built. Your faith in God and His Word must be the primary guide by which you steer through the challenges and oppositions you will face as a leader. It will give you the strength to stand firm when others falter and the wisdom to make decisions that are in line with God's will even when people may not like you for it, or even threaten you for it. Colossians 2:6-7 says

"As ye have therefore received Christ Jesus the Lord, so walk ye in him: Rooted and built up in him, and stablished in the faith, as ye have been taught, abounding therein with thanksgiving."

This rootedness in Christ is what will sustain you and enable you to be the generational force that God has called you to be so do not ever in any way joke with it or play with it.

In essence, becoming a generational embodiment of God's glory in leadership through which His blessings can flow to the world is a high calling. By embracing it, you become not just a recipient of God's blessings but a conduit through which His intentions can permeate the world. This is the essence of authentic leadership, one that leaves a lasting legacy and shapes the course of history according to God's divine plan.

Cultivating A Divine Mindset In The Face Of Opposition

Cultivating And Leading With A Divine Mindset

When you finally accept the responsibility that comes with being a global leader, global empowerer, and a generational blessing to the world, one of the strongholds that you must do battle with is the stronghold of worldly mindsets that have caged a lot of people in the world, even in the church. But how can you confront and defeat a worldly mindset if you do not have your divine mindset? God wants you to have a divine mindset so you can use your ideas effectively; this divine mindset is not something that comes naturally; it is cultivated through consistent communion with God, immersing yourself in His Word, and a deliberate choice to view the world through the lens of God's truth every single day of your life.

In truth, the moment you bring your ideas to the table, you should also expect opposition because the world is trained to fight anything that is of God and goes against the status quo of the devil. When you start telling your friends and family, *"I know this is how things should be done; this is how I want things done,"* they will oppose you. In school, they might even bully you or cast doubt on your ideas. But that's where leadership comes in. True leadership is not about avoiding opposition rather it is about standing firm in the face of it and shining the light of God towards it. You must have the courage to uphold your convictions even when everyone around you disagrees.

That's why I like the movie, *"The Chosen"* When Jesus was bringing His ideas to the world, some people opposed Him, saying, *"If you do this, you will be breaking the law of Moses."* But what did He say? He simply said, *"I am the law of Moses."* Wow! I love that! Jesus demonstrated the ultimate example of standing firm in the face of opposition; he did not shy away from conflict or compromise His message to appease His critics, no! and you must follow in his footsteps! He boldly proclaimed the truth, even when it was unpopular and mostly misunderstood.

If you have not seen The Chosen, you probably make it a family affair. Just sit down with your family and it together. Do not waste time on those Hollywood movies that try to sell you silly ideas; instead, turn to something that will inspire you and instill godly values in your spirit. Remember I earlier said you have to be intentional with the influences you allow into your life, now you must also be intentional about that of your loved ones too. Always choose the right contents, which are divine and will help you develop your mindset in line with God's intentions. I really do not understand why so many Christians keep gravitating toward bad influences. Until you are very strong, do not expose yourself to things that could corrupt your mind even if your intent is to change or correct them. This is an advice for cultivating a divine mindset. Just as you are careful about what you eat to maintain your physical health, you must also be equally vigilant about what you feed your mind. The media you consume, the conversations you engage in, and the company you keep all have a great impact on your mindset so choose wisely, and surround yourself with influences that strengthen you in Christ and reinforces your godly values.

There was a time when out of all my friends, I was the youngest in the group, but my stance on loyalty to our spiritual father was always superior and so I faced opposition because of it. Some pastors even called me a *"poster boy"* because of my level of loyalty, and I said, *"You can call me a slave if you like, if you ask me to be a houseboy and clean his toilet, I will do it."* They thought I had lost my mind, but I know I'm a leader; I knew God had great plans for me, and I knew a leader must serve! Thank God I'm both a natural king and a spiritual king so there is nothing earthly that will diminish me from who I am. It is the same with you; when you begin to follow the true principles of global leadership and a divine mindset, there are many people who will call you foolish and attempt to ridicule you in so many ways, but do not worry just stay committed in wherever God has placed you, and serve with all your heart even when others mock or misunderstand you. At the end of the day, this is how you will be able to cultivate the divine mindset needed to stand the fires of opposition when you finally stand as a leader who chooses to represent God and operate by Godly principles.

I know the convictions God has instilled in me. I realize that standing for truth can be difficult, but eventually, truth always wins. Sometimes I had no money for transportation to church, and my friends would say *"You are crazy! That's not how you do things, why not just use your offering as transportation even the Lord understands your heart"* But I as far as I was concerned, that was completely unacceptable; while growing up I was trained to know it is wrong to appear before the Lord empty-handed. So instead of using my offering for transport, I would rather walk to church, ensuring I had something to give to God. At that time, my offering was just five Naira, but I had a divine mindset, a mindset that prioritized God above all else, and I knew I must stand with the lord even if it was not favorable. This is the doggedness you need as a leader! Five naira is quite little now, but as of then, it meant a lot of money and was very significant to me. My friends laughed at me, called me names, and felt I was awkward, but today, there's none of them whose wealth and success come close to 25% of my abundance, and I am not just talking about money; I am a blessed man in every sense of the word, far beyond any form of material or physical prosperity. Does this mean I am better than them? Not necessarily, but it only means I was wise enough to function with a divine mindset.

In the end, following the right principles always pays off; I am a generational leader today because, through that same divine mindset, the Lord keeps using me to make an impact. Beloved, your friends may disagree with your philosophy, but if your philosophy is rooted in Christ and his mindset, stand firm because that is how you will operate in the divine mindset. Let your resilience shine through, soon the aura of your determination will begin to spread, and those who oppose you will find themselves sinking. And you know what? The more they sink, the more they will realize, "Look at this person walking on water and not sinking, he must know something, or she must know something that we do not know." By the time they get to this point, they will soon begin to value your mindset and ideology because they will realize that divinity is at work in you.

Learning From Daniels's Example (How To Cultivate The Divine Mindset)

This principle of standing firm in the face of opposition is beautifully illustrated in the life of Daniel, when you read the book of Daniel, you will see that although facing threats and persecution, he was a man who remained steadfast in his faith and convictions. Daniel 6:10 says it this way:

> "Now when Daniel knew that the writing was signed, he went into his house; and his windows being open in his chamber toward Jerusalem, he kneeled upon his knees three times a day, and prayed, and gave thanks before his God, as he did aforetime."

Daniel's unshakable commitment to his faith, even in the face of potential death, is a powerful example of the strength and courage of a divine mindset.

Now, to cultivate a divine mindset, you will require more than just knowledge of God's Word, you must have a very deep and personal relationship with His. I am talking about an intense level of intimacy with the father that goes beyond the average Christianity we see in many places.

Do you remember I talked about influences earlier? It also applies here. You will never have a divine mindset if you keep allowing the trivialities and corruptions of this world to pollute your mind. This means that you must guard your heart and mind against negativity and doubt or the enemy will use objects like discouragement, fear, depression, etc. to shake your faith and distort your perspective. This is why Philippians 4:8 says

> *"Finally, brethren, whatsoever things are true, whatsoever things are honest, whatsoever things are just, whatsoever things are pure, whatsoever things are lovely, whatsoever things are of good report; if there be any virtue, and if there be any praise, think on these things."*

By consistently focusing on what is good, pure, and praiseworthy, we strengthen our divine mindset and become less susceptible to the enemy's tactics.

Also, to cultivate a divine mindset effectively, you must develop a kingdom perspective on every aspect of your life. This means that you must view your career, relationships, finances, and even your challenges through God's eternal purposes. This means asking yourself, *"How can this situation be used for God's glory?"* or *"What is God trying to teach me through this?"* This perspective will allow you to rise above temporary setbacks and focus on the bigger picture of God's plan for your life and the world around you.

As you continue to stand firm and cultivate this divine mindset, I pray that God will grant you greater access to lead people, guide people, and continually expand your influence for the Kingdom's sake, in the mighty name of Jesus. I pray that people will be drawn to the peace, wisdom, and strength emanating from your life and leadership in the mighty name of Jesus.

Unshakeable Leadership

Defeating Worldly Influences With God's Wisdom

Never should you disdain your walk with God just to please your friends; never should you compromise your walk with God just to gain approval from your husband or wife. You must have this commitment to God above all else in this world. When you become this loyal to the lord, you have found one of the true pillars of unshakeable leadership that can impact the world and forever make you remain a transgenerational blessing. We are talking about recognizing that your primary allegiance is to God, and all other relationships should flow from and be guided by this primary relationship.

Do not forget, you are not smarter than Adam. When was the last time you successfully named animals that had no names? When was the last time you prophetically stood on the seashore and named an aquatic mammal, for example, looking at one and saying, *"You are a jellyfish"?* This should give you an idea concerning the revelation with which Adam's creativity operated; he operated at a divine frequency! So, if Adam could fall, then you need to be careful and recognize your need for divine wisdom every day. Just as Adam's ability to name the animals came from his intimate connection with God, our ability to lead effectively must also come from the Lord.

Now, just in case you are in a relationship but your boyfriend or girlfriend, husband or wife, is already giving you signs of deception and deceit, lying as if they live with Satan, then I want you to know things have to change, it is better for them to love you enough not to lie, than to fear you so much that they begin to lie. As a leader, you must create an environment where truth is valued and deception is not tolerated. It is far worse for them to lie all because they fear what you may do. You might think you are gaining respect, but ultimately, you are creating an environment where the light God wanted to shine in your life is turned against you. Authentic leadership does not go about instilling fear in people, rather it goes about inspiring people to embrace truth and integrity because it values creating an atmosphere where honesty is cherished and practiced, not out of fear, but out of respect for God and one another.

Just by choosing to be with God, you will stir up so many challenges, and see many people trying to destroy your philosophy using the wisdom of men. That's why you must stand your ground in leadership by refusing to chicken out. The world will always try to impose its wisdom on you, but you must stand firm as a leader grounded in God's wisdom. The Apostle Paul emphasized this in 1 Corinthians 3:19-20,

> *"For the wisdom of this world is foolishness with God. For it is written, He taketh the wise in their own craftiness. And again, The Lord knoweth the thoughts of the wise, that they are vain."*

This verse is a reminder that true wisdom comes from God, and it is this divine wisdom that we must rely on as we navigate the challenges of leadership in a world that often opposes godly principles.

This is why the Bible says Having done all to stand, Stand! You will be opposed but stand firm. We are all walking on water, but after a while, the wind will reveal those who truly have the truth within them. Either the water will swallow you, or you will defeat the water, making it serve you. Do you remember Peter? When Peter kept his eyes on Jesus, he could do the impossible, but when he looked at the waves, he began to sink; as leaders, we must keep our focus on God, trusting in His wisdom and power, even when the storms of opposition rage around us.

Lead The World With Your Success

In order to defeat worldly influences God wants you to lead the world with your success. This means you must find out the keys to being successful, and this lies in pursuing and following the plan of God for your life. in Joshua 1:8, the Lord said:

> *"This book of the law shall not depart out of thy mouth, but thou shalt meditate therein day and night, that thou mayest observe to do according to all that is written therein: for then thou shalt make thy way prosperous, and then thou shalt have success."*

This verse is a scripture that captures the importance of positioning our lives in line with God's Word as the foundation for true success. Being filled with the word of God, and His ways, and meditating on it day and night is not something you can bargain if you are truly serious about defeating the worldly opposition that the enemy will send you. If you fail, you have chosen that you are not ready to be the leader of impact that will shine the light for many others to see and follow.

Lead The World With Your Finances

God does not like it when a believer is broke because it turns you into a borrower instead of a lender thereby contradicting the scripture which tells us you are to go from increase to increase, strength to strength, glory to glory, power to power and that though your beginning may be small, as you progressively serve God, you will continue to increase. Financial prosperity is a form of prosperity that we truly cannot ignore or joke about in any way, it is a primary tool for the advancement of God's kingdom. When God blesses you financially, you must realize that money in the hands of a leader is a great power that must be used wisely. Through it you can either build or destroy, the choice is yours. But know that God brought that money into your hands so you can break the cycle of poverty in your life and then in the lives of many people as much as possible, through providing hope, help, encouragement, and comfort for those in need.

Never Neglect God

You must stay hooked up to God at all costs as a leader. Do not worry about people just focus on God. Like I said earlier, when you believe God's word it will shape your ideology and create your philosophy of life, and because you are different the world will try to tell you it is not good to serve God this way. They will say you are praying too much or attending church too much. Why attend three services? They will claim you do not have a life, but who told you that? What kind of life are you looking for? This questioning of worldly standards is crucial for unshakeable leadership; you must be willing to go against the grain of societal norms when they conflict with God's standards.

Some people do not even go to church from Monday to Friday, and then on Sunday, instead of completely dedicating themselves to the presence of God, they just want to rush in and rush out of church. Well, you will never become the leader or the man God intended that way. They should get lost in the house of God, attending two or three services to solidify their destinies. If you are living such a careless life, then you do not know what you are doing; the challenges ahead will humble you because these are seasons where we are witnessing a clash of powers with satanic raging at its worst.

Let me round up this chapter by bringing to your notice once again that unshakeable leadership rooted in God's wisdom is about standing firm in your convictions, even when the world opposes you; leading with integrity, pursuing God's plan for your life, and using your success and finances to advance His kingdom. It demands a heightened level of commitment to spiritual growth also, and a willingness to go against worldly wisdom as well as cultivating a deep trust in God's principles. With these qualities in place, I assure you that you truly will become a leader who not only withstands the storms of opposition but also influences the world for God's glory. And do not forget, true leadership is not in you conforming to the world's standards, but in you transforming the world through the blessings of God upon your life and being steadfast in God's truth and love.

CHAPTER FIVE

BLESSED WITH POWER

◆ ◆ ◆

"A life without power is limited, but with God's supernatural strength, you will achieve beyond human expectations."

◆ ◆ ◆

Achieve, Protect, And Lead
With God's Strength

Understanding Power

Many believers live a powerless life, and this is completely against God's intention for all of us. The Lord wants you to be filled with supernatural power, surging and breaking out through you. A man without power is a greatly limited man. There is financial power, relationship power (connections), physical power (human strength), emotional power, and all other classes of power, but do you know what the strongest and most unbeatable power is? IT IS SPIRITUAL POWER. When this power lands in your life, you become far more than an ordinary human being, and this is God's ultimate desire for you.

When spiritual power rests upon your life from God, so many things will immediately become possible because God's power infuses you with strength, ensuring that you do not wake up each day feeling sick, tired, or mentally weak. Instead, the power of God enters your life and takes over, empowering you to wake up refreshed even after only a few hours of sleep. You may work long hours and still feel stronger than those who rested for much longer. This supernatural energy defies human logic and understanding, for it is not of this world but from the very throne of God Himself. This infusion brings about a stability in your life that is unshakeable thereby making your journey toward destiny no longer a journey of endless and painful struggles.

With this infusion of strength, you do not crawl into your purpose or creep along like a rat, No! You walk into your destiny majestically, with the confidence of one who knows their God and the power He has bestowed upon them. As the Scripture declares in Isaiah 40:31,

> "But they that wait upon the Lord shall renew their strength; they shall mount up with wings as eagles; they shall run, and not be weary; and they shall walk, and not faint."

This is the promise of God for those who tap into His supernatural power and do you know what? This is heavily available to you today!

Think of the lion, the king of the jungle, does it cower around like a helpless animal begging for help and survival? NO! It stands strong and fearless, not shrinking away from any challenge, this is the true portrait of a believer filled with God's power, even people who talk about you may not understand your life, but while they are gossiping and speculating, you are being strengthened in the spirit, growing in might and stature before the Lord. And each time there is an opportunity for you to show up, they will be left speechless, saying, *"We thank God for your life,"* realizing that despite their words and doubts, you have risen above all expectations and your life is now and forever a testament to the power of God just like the bible says in Ephesians 3:20,

> *"Now unto him that is able to do exceeding abundantly above all that we ask or think, according to the power that worketh in us."*

It is through this power that you will be able to influence the world for God even beyond several dimensions which we have been discussing and in line with the command of Matthew 5:14-16

> *"Ye are the light of the world. A city that is set on an hill cannot be hid. Neither do men light a candle, and put it under a bushel, but on a candlestick; and it giveth light unto all that are in the house. Let your light so shine before men, that they may see your good works, and glorify your Father which is in heaven."*

Look at this call again, take your time to meditate on it, and from the bottom of your heart I want you to say *"Lord I accept the call!"*

There are three major aspects of power that God wants you to harness so that you can make a significant impact through His spirit:

- **The Power to Achieve**

The first aspect of God's power is the power to achieve anything you desire according to His will. People may say, *"This mountain cannot be crossed; this cannot be done."* But when you feel the weight of those doubts, you must go back in the spirit. Suddenly, the Spirit of God will speak to you, saying, *"Not by might, nor by power, but by My Spirit."* before you know it, this powerful declaration from Zechariah 4:6 will then become your battle cry, and your source of confidence in the face of terrible obstacles that would have crushed any other person

I want you to declare right now, *"I have received the word of God, and Because of His Spirit, I will succeed!"* Then turn to those mountains again that may have defeated you before and confront them with renewed strength. Do you not know that the same Spirit that raised Christ from the dead now dwells in you? It constantly empowers you to overcome any challenge that stands in your way so that you can also boldly declare, as Paul did in Philippians 4:13,

> *"I can do all things through Christ which strengtheneth me."*

When the world doubts your ability to accomplish your goals, you should know that through God's power, you can indeed rise above, and they will start seeking your God because your life will become a living testimony to the power of faith and the might of the Almighty. Suddenly, people will look at you and wonder, *"What is the source of his strength? How can he achieve so much in the face of such adversity?"* And you will have the privilege of pointing them to the one trustworthy source of all power, the living God.

I prophesy that you will be a beacon in your generation and a generational blessing because you are providing leadership through your achievements and I declare that the power of God will support you in every endeavor, causing you to excel beyond human expectations in the mighty name of Jesus. As you step out in faith, tackling projects and pursuits that others deem impossible, I decree that the hand of God goes before you, making crooked paths straight and rough places smooth in the mighty name of Jesus

No matter what you may be struggling to achieve today, meditate on Isaiah 45:2,

> *"I will go before thee, and make the crooked places straight: I will break in pieces the gates of brass, and cut in sunder the bars of iron."*

Child of God, you are an achiever because the power of the Most High rests upon you. No goal is too lofty, and no dream is too significant when walking in God's power. So why not step out in faith again, knowing that He who called you is faithful and will bring to pass every good work He has purposed for your life?

• The Protective Power of God:

The second aspect of God's power that must be evident in your life is His protective power. When you begin to rise and achieve great things for the Kingdom, and when people begin to see the blessing of God actively working upon your life, many weapons will be formed against you. But fear not, for God, has already said in Isaiah 54:17, that No weapon that is formed against thee shall prosper; and every tongue that shall rise against thee in judgment you will condemn. When people attempt to attack you, and God's protective power is upon your life, they will soon realize that you, are too guarded to be defeated. King David was a man who faced numerous enemies and challenges, yet he testified to this protective power in Psalm 18:3 by saying,

> *"I will call upon the Lord, who is worthy to be praised: so shall I be saved from mine enemies."*

Those who come against do not have the license to touch you, and as long as this revelation is in your spirit, they will soon discover that fighting you is a death sentence for them and a suicide mission for those who send them. This is how the power of God operates in the life of those who enjoy his blessings. We are surrounded by a hedge of protection that no enemy can penetrate.

When the enemy rises against you, they are on a self-destructive path because you are not the type to be easily fought or gossiped about. Your strength lies not in your own abilities, but in the, mighty hand of God that upholds you. Do you remember the story of Elisha? When they sent soldiers to arrest him, his servant began to panic and became very worried. Why? Because the servant had not been taught about God's protective power as I am teaching you now. But what did Elisha do? He calmly said to the worried servant *"Fear not: for they that be with us are more than they that be with them."* 2 Kings 6:16. Do you not know that those who are with you are more than those who are against you?

When God finally opened the servant's eyes and he saw chariots of fire surrounding them, all his fear and worry finally died. That's the exact same thing the Lord is doing to you right now, you may have been worried about situations, circumstances, and attacks but right now He is opening your eyes and he is saying to you *"They that are with you are more than those against you"*. With a single word, Elisha prayed, *"Father, blind them!"* and all the attackers became blind captives of Elisha and his servant instead of capturing him. This is the same protective power that is available to you today so no matter what forces gangs up against you, whether seen or unseen you can rest and be assured that the Lord of Hosts fights on your behalf. This is why I can boldly say to you that even the plans of your enemies can turn to your advantage and what was meant for evil, God will turn for your good; Your life will also become a living testament to the words of Romans 8:31, *"What shall we then say to these things? If God be for us, who can be against us?"* Let this truth sink deep into your spirit, and walk in the confidence that comes from knowing you are divinely protected.

- **The Power to Lead:**

I have talked about some aspects of leadership in the previous chapter, but let us now look at another dimension. Many people make the mistake of thinking leadership is a natural thing, but it is not! Look at Moses, David, and Solomon; did any of them succeed in leadership naturally? No, they all required divine empowerment to lead effectively. Though educated in all the wisdom of Egypt, Moses needed a divine encounter at the burning bush to become the leader God called him to be. How about David? Well, David was a mere shepherd boy, but he was anointed (a sign of empowerment) by Prophet Samuel to lead Israel, and because of this empowerment, Saul could not kill Him, the Philistines could not kill him, even when His son was after his life, they still failed. It is almost as though he was indestructible; why? Because the power to lead was at work in his life.

Have you also thought of Solomon? Solomon was just a normal man; in fact, his mother came into the palace through one of the most grievous sins of David, his father, however after offering sacrifices to the Lord, God was moved to ask him what he wanted; Solomon knew that he couldn't ask for natural things or mundane prosperity so he asked for supernatural wisdom, this was where he received the power to lead, let us read it 1 Kings 3:7-9:

> "And now, O Lord my God, thou hast made thy servant king instead of David my father: and I am but a little child: I know not how to go out or come in. And thy servant is in the midst of the people whom thou hast chosen, a great people who cannot be numbered nor counted for multitude. Give therefore thy servant an understanding heart to judge thy people, that I may discern between good and bad: for who is able to judge this thy so great a people?"

Is not that amazing? Just look up to God today and tell him that you want this. You do not have to wait for a vision, you can ask in faith and the Lord will answer you.

> Psalm 144:1-2 says, "Blessed be the Lord my strength, which teacheth my hands to war, and my fingers to fight: My goodness, and my fortress; my high tower, and my deliverer; my shield, and he in whom I trust; who subdueth my people under me."

I brought this scripture out again, to reemphasize the fact that as long as you are a leader, there will be enemies, terrible enemies, and these are not just humans alone, but also spirits. But when the power to lead is active in your life, then you will tear them down because you are already far above them, and God's might is flowing through you.

The power to lead is not just about having authority over others; it is about having the wisdom, discernment, and strength to guide people toward God's purpose. It is you being able to hold your ground against all forces of darkness in your territory and the life of those close to you so that everyone connected to you can progress in line with God's intention for them. As a leader empowered by God, you are the only hope some people will ever have if their lives are meaningful, so do not joke with this position and the empowerment God is releasing in your life. By walking in light of this revelation and empowerment, you will see that people will become naturally drawn to you; they will sense the anointing upon your life and the authority with which you speak and act; your words will carry weight, and your actions will inspire others to follow Christ also. All these dimensions of being blessed increase and are part of your inheritance in Christ.

What Does It Take To Become A True Spiritual

Leader

To become a true spiritual leader, you must first and foremost stand firm in your faith, as the Apostle Paul tells us in 1 Corinthians 16:13,

> *"Watch ye, stand fast in the faith, quit you like men, be strong."*

This steadfastness is vital because, in your strength, you will fall. It is God's power that brings both the offensive and defensive presence of God, thereby giving you a level of boldness that surpasses human understanding, a level of strength to win all battles, a level of wisdom to act and get results, and so many other elements also.

My spiritual father will always say, *"When you see an antelope charging at you, you need to check what is backing it up; when a goat or a sheep confronts an elephant or a hyena, you should look around; there something is backing it up"* This principle is the true power behind spiritual leadership. In yourself, you are just an ordinary man, so if you attempt to be a blessing to the world against the will of the devil who has held them in chains and bondage then you can be sure that the enemy will beat you up, chew you and spit out your bones. But this can never happen to a true spiritual leader who has been blessed to proliferate because all the dimensions of God's power which we have earlier discussed are at work in Him. In other words, on your journey of being a true spiritual leader who wants to see the world blessed just as you have been blessed to proliferate, your boldness and courage in attacking the devil and breaking people from his bondage must come not from your abilities, but from the mighty God who stands behind you.

Think about David confronting Goliath, do you think that was normal? When David saw Goliath he charged towards him, but when Saul, who was supposed to be the giant of Israel because of

His height, saw him, he crawled like a chicken; even when David came to him that he would take down Goliath, Saul quickly said get this guy down, you are just a tiny boy, But David replied with confidence,

> *"And David said unto Saul, Thy servant kept his father's sheep, and there came a lion and a bear, and took a lamb out of the flock: And I went out after him, and smote him, and delivered it out of his mouth: and when he arose against me, I caught him by his beard, and smote him, and slew him. Thy servant slew both the lion and the bear: and this uncircumcised Philistine shall be as one of them, seeing he hath defied the armies of the living God. David said moreover, The Lord that delivered me out of the paw of the lion and out of the bear's paw, he will deliver me out of the hand of this Philistine. And Saul said unto David, Go, and the Lord be with thee." 1 Samuel 17:34-37.*

This response shows that his confidence was not in his strength but in God's power and God's faithfulness.

Do Not Trust The Weapons Of Men Above God's Power In Your Life

As a spiritual leader, you cannot afford to trust in the natural weapons and tactics of men above God, if you do this you will fail; you will never be able to step into God's blessings for your life or even be able to lead other out from bondage into God's intended blessings for them. Let me show you something in 1 Samuel 17:38-39 the bible says

> *"And Saul armed David with his armour, and he put an helmet of brass upon his head; also he armed him with a*

coat of mail. And David girded his sword upon his armor, and he assayed to go; for he had not proved it. And David said unto Saul, I cannot go with these; for I have not proved them. And David put them off him."

David chose to trust in God's power rather than the armor and weapons of the king, feeling that he was more equipped with his faith and experience as a shepherd than with unfamiliar military equipment, and He went on to face Goliath with only his sling, stones, and trust in God.

David's strength came not from anything physical but from a true spiritual leader who can bring the people into God's blessing by taking down the enemy; his strength came from his faith in the God of Israel. This is why he said in 1 Samuel 17:45,

"Thou comest to me with a sword, and with a spear, and with a shield: but I come to thee in the name of the Lord of hosts, the God of the armies of Israel, whom thou hast defied."

The Strength Of Man Will Fail

I tell you the truth: trying to overwork yourself in your strength does not work; it will not produce the result you are looking for, and I promise you such acts of trying to fight with human strength in the face of satanic agendas will always fail. I have seen many pastors and am shocked at how easily it is for some to be so neutral and indifferent concerning the power of God. Some of them genuinely want their church to grow, but if all you have to develop your church is human strength and endeavors, then you can be sure that even if you somehow gather people, eventually, they will look for truth and leave you. Even the workers in that church will not be able to withstand demons so that they will be oppressed, and when demons begin to oppress them, what will they do? They will probably look for counselors.

It is such a shame that many people think all that they need is just therapy. Do not be foolish; you will spill your heart and mind to someone who does not even know God just because they have a psychology degree. What philosophy led to their psychology degree? Some people say they are counselors, but they need counseling themselves, yet you will share your heart with them. Before you know it, they will take everything you say and send it straight to Satan or any demonic agents through which the enemy can oppress your life. I am not saying counseling is terrible. Instead, I am saying you need spirit-filled counselors.

The excellent news is that I am thanking God that they are available in the body of Christ. I am talking about counselors who are filled with the Holy Ghost. Do you know the unique part? You can also be one! Yes, you can be a counselor filled with the Holy Spirit because people need help; they need genuine counseling. But you can't go to a devil to cast out a devil. As Jesus said in Matthew 12:26,

> "And if Satan cast out Satan, he is divided against himself; how shall then his kingdom stand?"

No matter how experienced a psychologist or psychiatrist may be, they can never cast out a demon using psychology. You need power, the anointing to cast out devils, and the signature of God's authority in your life.

So, God has given you His power; understand that this generation needs you; the lion is the strongest, not the biggest. You do not have to be big; you just have to be strong in the Lord! Being assertive also means being brave among the beasts; do not let anything hold you back! No more crawling into your destiny. You have been blessed to increase, and it is time to fully walk in that blessing so that as a true spiritual leader, you can also lead others into their blessings.

Let Go Of Fear

Sometimes, you may want to declare your prophecy, but fear holds you back, and you will begin to think, *"What if I tell people what God wants to do in my life, and they try to kill my prophecy, or what if I tell them and then it does not happen, won't I be ashamed?"* Well, thank God for the days they may have succeeded in killing any prophecies of your life, but now that the Lord is opening your eyes and you are reading this, know that those days are over.

I want you to know that you can declare your prophecy and will not stop achieving it! You will speak your prophecy boldly and have the power to ensure that anyone who tries to stop it will die. Look at Acts 13:11,

> *"And now, behold, the hand of the Lord is upon thee, and thou shalt be blind, not seeing the sun for a season. And immediately there fell on him a mist and a darkness, and he went about seeking some to lead him by the hand."*

This was a demonic agent trying to ruin Paul's endeavors as he went about his destiny and assignment. Paul did not suddenly start crying and begging instead he gave a declaration of authority and immediately the devilish agent became blind. I am not just talking about Paul; I am saying you can do the same because the blessings of the Lord are upon you!

Some uncommon things you must commit yourself to as a spiritual leader so you can truly enjoy being blessed as well as constantly remain a blessing to everyone around your sphere.

- **Uncompromising Pursuit of Holiness**

A true spiritual leader must commit to an uncompromising pursuit of holiness beyond mere outward appearance or adherence to rules; I am saying that you must cultivate a heart wholly devoted to God. As the Scripture says in 1 Peter 1:15-16,

> "But as he which hath called you is holy, so be ye holy in all manner of conversation; Because it is written, Be ye holy; for I am holy."

This commitment to holiness requires constant vigilance and self-examination. It means being willing to confront and root out any area of sin or compromise in your life, no matter how small or hidden it may seem. It involves daily dying to self and a continual yielding to the sanctifying work of the Holy Spirit. Also, this pursuit of holiness should be evident in every aspect of your life, such as your thoughts, words, actions, and relationships. It should influence your business dealings, family life, and private moments when no one is watching. As a spiritual leader, your life becomes an open book, and people will look to you as an example of godly living. Therefore, you must be able to say with Paul,

> "Be ye followers of me, even as I also am of Christ" (1 Corinthians 11:1).

• Sacrificial Love for God's People (200 words):

A true spiritual leader must commit to a sacrificial love for God's people; this is a king of love that goes beyond mere sentiment or good feelings. A love willing to lay down one's life for the flock, just as Christ did for the Church. As Jesus said in John 15:13,

> "Greater love hath no man than this, that a man lay down his life for his friends."

You see, this sacrificial love means putting the needs of others before your own. It means being available to counsel, comfort, and guide even when it is inconvenient or costly to you personally. It means rejoicing with those who rejoice and weeping with those who weep (Romans 12:15).

You should also have it at heart that this love should be impartial and unconditional because, as a spiritual leader, you must love the unlovable, reach out to the outcasts, and show compassion to the difficult ones in your congregation. Your love should reflect God's love - patient, kind, not easily angered, keeping no record of wrongs (1 Corinthians 13:4-5). This sacrificial will also demand discipline when necessary because Proverbs 27:5 says, *"Open rebuke is better than secret love."* As a true spiritual leader, you must also love God and people enough to correct them when they are straying. Do not say because you love them; you do not want to fix them because it may hurt their feelings. Instead, you should always do so with the goal of restoration and growth, not shame or disgrace the offender.

- **Relentless Commitment to Prayer and Intercession:**

Let us talk about prayer once more; I talk about this in almost everything because, for a spiritual man, prayer is an absolute necessity, and as a spiritual leader, you must commit yourself to a relentless life of prayer and intercession. Know it and never forget that prayer is not just a religious duty; it is the lifeblood of spiritual leadership. Even Jesus Himself demonstrated that effective ministry flows from a vibrant prayer life. Luke 5:16 says, *"And he withdrew himself into the wilderness, and prayed."* This commitment to prayer means prioritizing that you must prioritize and always have special times alone with God, especially praying in tongues as led by the spirit of God, even amid busy schedules and pressing demands.

A good and excellent example was Moses standing in the gap for Israel (Exodus 32:11-14). You must be willing to wrestle in prayer for those under your care, and this also means praying for their spiritual growth, protection from the enemy, and for God's purposes to be fulfilled in their lives.

Unshakable Commitment To Biblical Truth

As a spiritual leader, you cannot afford not to have an unbending commitment to Biblical truth and bible study. Yes, there may be days you do not feel like studying, but commitment means you must still do it even if you do not. In today's world of relativism and watered-down gospel messages, you have to stand firm on the unchanging Word of God just as Paul exhorted Timothy in 2 Timothy 4:2-4,

> *"Preach the word; be instant in season, out of season; reprove, rebuke, exhort with all longsuffering and doctrine. For the time will come when they will not endure sound doctrine; after their lusts shall they heap to themselves teachers, having itching ears; And they shall turn away their ears from the truth, and shall be turned unto fables."*

Note this: Your commitment to truth means diligently studying the Scriptures, rightly dividing the word of truth (2 Timothy 2:15), and being willing to preach the whole counsel of God, even when certain truths may be unpopular or challenging. You will also have to accept the mantle of guarding against false doctrines and teachings that may creep into the church from the pits of hell.

6 Pitfalls You Must Guard Against To Be A True Spiritual Leader And A Generational Blessing

· **Immoral Sins Such as Fornication or Adultery:**

These things affect your spirit and pollute your body as the temple of God, so as a spiritual leader, you must guard vigilantly against sexual immorality. Realize that the enemy knows that if he can cause you to fall in this area, he can potentially destroy your ministry and bring reproach to the name of Christ. Paul warns in 1 Corinthians 6:18-20,

> *"Flee fornication. Every sin a man doeth is without the body; but he that committeth fornication sinneth against his own body. What? Know ye not that your body is the temple of the Holy Ghost which is in you, which ye have of God, and ye are not your own? For ye are bought with a price: therefore glorify God in your body and spirit, which is God's."*

Now, guarding against sexual immorality involves more than just avoiding physical acts; it also includes protecting your eyes, your thoughts, and your heart. Job 31:1 says, "I made a covenant with mine eyes; why should I think upon a maid?" This means being careful about what you watch, read, or listen to. It means setting clear boundaries in your interactions with the opposite sex.

· Bitterness and Anger

Bitterness and anger are also silent killers of spiritual leadership because they can poison your spirit, cloud your judgment, and hinder your ability to love and lead God's people effectively. Hebrews 12:15 says, *"Looking diligently lest any man fail of the grace of God; lest any root of bitterness springing up trouble you, and thereby many be defiled."*

As a spiritual leader, it is true that you will face situations that could potentially lead to bitterness or anger such as disappointments, betrayals, criticism, and even unfair treatment, but the truth remains that you must guard your heart against these negative emotions. Remember the words of Paul in Ephesians 4:31-32,

"Let all bitterness, and wrath, and anger, and clamor, and evil speaking, be put away from you, with all malice: And be ye kind one to another, tenderhearted, forgiving one another, even as God for Christ's sake hath forgiven you."

Guarding against bitterness and anger also means you will have to cultivate a spirit of forgiveness and grace and always choose to bless and pray for those who mistreat you (Luke 6:28).

- **Greediness and Always Wanting to Collect People's Money**

The love of money is the root of all kinds of evil, and as a spiritual leader, you must guard against the temptation of greed. 1 Timothy 6:10-11 warns,

"For the love of money is the root of all evil: which while some coveted after, they have erred from the faith, and pierced themselves through with many sorrows. But thou, O man of God, flee these things; and follow after righteousness, godliness, faith, love, patience, meekness."

Although it is biblical for ministers to receive financial support (1 Corinthians 9:14), it becomes problematic when pursuing money becomes a primary motivation. Guard against the temptation to manipulate or pressure people into giving. Remember, God loves a cheerful giver (2 Corinthians 9:7), not one who gives out of compulsion or guilt.

Instead of focusing on collecting money, focus on faithfully teaching God's Word and caring for His people and trust that as you seek first His kingdom and righteousness, He will provide for your needs (Matthew 6:33). You should also be transparent and accountable in financial matters so that you can ensure all monetary dealings in your ministry are above reproach. Peter encourages us in 1 Peter 5:2, saying,

"Feed the flock of God which is among you, taking the oversight thereof, not by constraint, but willingly; not for filthy lucre, but of a ready mind."

• Over Busyness:

In the pursuit of ministry goals and the desire to serve God's people, I have seen many spiritual leaders fall into the trap of over-busyness; I mean, they become so consumed with doing things for God that they neglect their relationship with God and this is a very terrible and dangerous pitfall that usually leads to burnout, spiritual dryness, and ultimately, ineffective leadership. Do you remember the story of Mary and Martha in Luke 10:38-42? When Martha was *"cumbered about much serving,"* Mary chose to sit at Jesus' feet and listen to His word. Jesus commended Mary by saying she had chosen the *"good part."* As a spiritual leader, you must prioritize your time with God above all else. No amount of activity can substitute for intimacy with Christ.

To achieve this, you must maintain a healthy balance between ministry work and personal spiritual nourishment, so set boundaries on your time and learn to say no to good things that could distract you from the best things. And then, regularly take time for solitude and silence so you can allow God to refresh and refill you. Isaiah 40:31:

"But they that wait upon the Lord shall renew their strength; they shall mount up with wings as eagles; they shall run, and not be weary; and they shall walk, and not faint."

• Pride and Self-Reliance:

Pride is a terrible and dangerous pitfall, in fact, it is not just a pitfall it is a spiritual killer for spiritual leaders. You really need to be careful because it can manifest in various ways such as thinking too highly of yourself, refusing to admit mistakes, being unteachable, or even relying on your strength and wisdom rather than God's. Proverbs 16:18

> *"Pride goeth before destruction, and a haughty spirit before a fall."*

As your ministry grows and you begin to see success, I caution against the temptation to take credit for what God has done. 1 Corinthians 4:7 says,

"For who maketh thee to differ from another? and what hast thou that thou didst not receive? Now, if thou didst receive it, why dost thou glory, as if thou hadst not received it?"

You should intentionally cultivate a spirit of humility and dependence on God by regularly acknowledging your need for His grace and guidance. Do not forget that the Bible says in James 4:6, *"God resisteth the proud, but giveth grace unto the humble."*

· Prioritize Your Feeding

While this looks almost the same as over business, which we discussed earlier, they are very different. Being over-busy means, you do not have time because your routine is choked, but certain people have the time but are lazy and sometimes do not prioritize their spiritual health. As a spiritual leader, it is easy to become so focused on feeding others that you neglect your spiritual nourishment. This dangerous pitfall can lead to spiritual stagnation and ineffective leadership. Remember, you cannot give what you do not have as a spiritual man. In 1 Timothy 4:15-16 the Bible says,

> *"Meditate upon these things; give thyself wholly to them; that thy profiting may appear to all. Take heed unto thyself*

*and the doctrine; continue in them: for in doing this thou
shalt both save thyself and them that hear thee."*

There is a profit that should appear in your life, but it will only
appear when you give yourself ultimately!

Also, you should be accountable to others for your spiritual
growth. Have mentors or peers who can challenge you, encourage
you, and help you grow. Remember, even as a leader, you are still a
disciple of Christ, always learning and growing in your faith.

· Compromise of Biblical Truth

In today's world, so many people claim to be correct, but within
their hearts, they know that they are simply bending the bible
truths to suit whatever they want to say. Being a spiritual leader
who the Lord is ordaining to change the lives of many people,
you will also face this temptation, and do not get me wrong;
you do not have to be a pastor to have some certain level
of spiritual leadership over people. Spiritual leaders always face
the temptation to compromise biblical truth, significantly when
they are in a tight position. This could involve watering down
the gospel message, avoiding *"controversial"* topics, or adjusting
biblical standards to fit your cultural norms. Nevertheless, no
matter what the case may be, as a true spiritual leader, you must
stand firm on the unchanging Word of God.

> *2 Timothy 4:3-4, "For the time will come when they will not
> endure sound doctrine; but after their lusts shall they heap
> to themselves teachers, having itching ears; And they shall
> turn away their ears from the truth, and shall be turned
> unto fables."*

Do not allow this pitfall to become the doom of your calling
as a generational blessing who has been blessed to carry God's
blessing to the present and future generations. Guide against

this by committing yourself to the whole counsel of God's Word, preaching the truth in love, and always being ready to defend the truth when needed. Remember, you are accountable to God, not people's opinions or cultural trends.

CHAPTER SIX

THE POWER OF
BEING SEPARATED

◆ ◆ ◆

"Separation from the familiar is not a setback; it is the stage where God prepares you to be the deliverer of your family."

◆ ◆ ◆

Learning From Joseph

Becoming The Chosen Vessel For Your Family's Future

By now, through our discussion, you must have gotten to the point where you realize that our lives are not merely our own but vessels through which God's blessings can flow to impact generations. This is the truth that once again is encapsulated in being a chosen vessel for your family's future. I need you to think for a moment about the weight of responsibility and the immense privilege of being selected by the Almighty to be a conduit of His grace and favor to your family and their future. This is a calling that demands our utmost attention and commitment. Yet, how often do we find ourselves entangled in the web of complaints and constantly being angry about our circumstances and the shortcomings of our family lineage?

The Word of God admonishes us in Philippians 2:14-15 that we are to do all things without murmurings and disputing, so that we may be blameless and harmless, the sons of God, without rebuke, amid a crooked and perverse nation, among whom ye shine as lights in the world. This scripture is a clarion call, urging us to rise above the temptation to complain and instead embrace our role as saviors and chosen vessels through which God can reach our families. Before we go further, you should know that the path to becoming a savior for your family is not built with ease and comfort. It will require a period of separation and isolation where God will mold and shape you into a vessel that he can genuinely use. This separation, although challenging, is vital if you are to fulfill this intention of God indeed.

Several accounts in the bible show us how God works when He chooses someone to bless a family; one such person is Joseph. God picked Joseph as an individual, and you must accept that you are the chosen one, too. Say it to yourself: "I am the chosen one." Do not be so scared of the fact that sometimes the one picked by God may be the one who goes through all the hell and high water for the sake of the family rather focus on the fact that, even in all that you may be going through or have to go through as the chosen one, if you do not master the art of navigation and staying with God all through the process, everything you endure may end up as a waste. I am saying, if you can't apply your experiences to your purpose and calling, the reason for which God gave you life, it will become a useless experience. But if you learn how to navigate correctly, you will be able to realize that your struggles are working together for your good.

Let Us Now Learn From The Life Of Joseph

The life of Joseph not only shows us how God separates people for greatness but also reveals that the path involves many challenges and obstacles to conquer. Joseph was a man favored by his father, Jacob, and Jacob truly loved the young boy. He even received a coat of many colors from his father, Jacob, symbolizing this favor (Genesis 37:3). Now, His brothers soon became driven by jealousy and sold him into slavery; before we know it, Joseph soon found himself in Egypt, wholly separated from his family, culture, and everything he had ever known. What is striking about Joseph's story is that throughout the various trials, slavery, false accusations, and imprisonment, Joseph was a man who remained connected to God's purpose. He understood that his suffering was not the end and that it was a part of the divine process to elevate him. When you look at your challenges, do you think this way, or are you constantly feeling like life is unfair? If you keep thinking that way, you will be blinded to the true miracles God is working out through those challenges. All you will ever do successfully will be to complain.

Joseph did not complain about his situation; he did not get bitter, and he never lost faith and hope in God as many Christians would have done in our day and time. Instead, he trusted God's hand in his circumstances and realized that the painful separation was necessary for God to use him to save his family. This is why he could boldly say in Genesis 50:20,

> *"But as for you, ye thought evil against me; but God meant it unto good, to bring to pass, as it is this day, to save much people alive."*

This should be a revelation to you that every trial, betrayal, and moment of despair is part of a larger plan for you and your family's deliverance.

Do Not Escape From Destiny

You may be struggling now, and it looks like things are not working, well do not worry; you are still in the making process, joseph was first a leader in Potiphar's house and then he became a leader in prison and then next thing we saw is that he became a leader in all of Egypt. This is Job 8:7 7 in action *"Though thy beginning was small, yet thy latter end should greatly increase."* What a powerful promise! Your current trials and situations may seem overwhelming, filling you with doubt about yourself and telling you are small. But I can assure you that if you stay faithful, the end of your story will be one of increase and victory, so do not despise your small beginnings and the challenges you are going through.

Imagine if Joseph escaped prison just like you are looking for shortcuts to get out of your current training ground (your challenges). Then, he never would have met the servant who introduced him to the Pharaoh, or maybe they would have gone to prison to fetch him, only to discover that he had escaped from prison. That is how many people think they are escaping from trials and training; they do not know that they are only escaping from destiny and sentencing their family members to unending sufferings and pains because the chosen one has decided to abort destiny.

Significant Reasons Why Separation Is Necessary In Preparation

- **Learning to Trust God Completely**

When you are separated from the familiar, particularly from people who may show you undue or due favor, you are forced to depend on God. Joseph was sold into slavery and thrown into prison, so he had no one else to turn to but God, and in that place of separation and loneliness, he had to learn to rely entirely on God's provision, wisdom, and timing. Similarly, when God separates you, it strips away every safety net of human approval, resources, or connections you may be relying on, so in separation, you are drawn closer to him. The goal of separation is not to leave you alone but to leave you alone with God. This forces you to develop an intimate relationship with God, trusting Him as your ultimate source of help and favor.

• Building Character through Adversity

Joseph's character was formed through the trials he endured during his separation. By being sold into slavery, wrongfully imprisoned, and constantly facing unjust treatment, he learned patience, humility, and integrity. These traits prepared him to handle the enormous responsibility of ruling Egypt and saving his family during the famine. Know that God will often separate us to build our character in ways that comfort and ease cannot. In these tough seasons, you will be able to develop traits like perseverance, self-control, and wisdom, ensuring that when you are given authority, you can lead with integrity, wisdom, and compassion. Without this character-building process, you may not be able to handle the weight of responsibility that comes with being a blessing to others.

• Spiritual Maturity

Separation provides the opportunity to develop spiritual maturity. In the silence and solitude, God often speaks most clearly, revealing truths about Himself, His plans, and your purpose. You see, Joseph had dreams from God even before his separation, but during his years of isolation, he grew to understand those dreams and how they were tied to his family's destiny. Initially, they all interpreted Joseph's dream within the context of his family bowing before him. Still, in his separation season, he understood that the dream was far beyond his family. This is because separation pushes you to spend more time praying, meditating on God's Word, and seeking divine direction.

· Preparation for Leadership

Leadership often requires a season of separation, where you are trained in obscurity before being elevated to a position of influence. Think about it, this is why you do not see princes and princesses walking and gallivanting around. It is like being in the military, where you can have concealed and trained for a season before you are then released to provide security and take care of the civilians. This is the exact same thing with isolation; this is a period where you are locked alone with God to be adequately prepared for leadership. Joseph was pampered all along in his father's house. But when he became a slave and separated from his father, as an enslaved person and prisoner he learned crucial skills such as managing resources, handling people, and making wise decisions, all of which he used when he was appointed as Egypt's second-in-command. In other words, your separation period allows you to hone your skills, get new skills, acquire necessary practical knowledge, develop the emotional intelligence necessary for leadership, and be a blessing and a deliverer to your family when God finally says you are ready.

· Gaining Perspective Away from Familiar Influences

Separation gives you a fresh perspective on your family, relationships and calling. Had Joseph stayed with his brothers and father, he might have been influenced by their jealousy or even conformed to their ways of thinking. Being separated allowed Joseph to see his life from a divine viewpoint, understanding his unique role in God's plan. Similarly, God may need to distance you from familiar surroundings so He can prevent negative influences from stunting your growth. Then, in isolation, you are more likely to receive a clearer vision of God's plan for your life and how it connects to being a blessing to your family.

Child of God, if you look at your life today and see the struggles, the challenges, the loneliness, and the separation, know this: God is setting you up for something far greater. Like Joseph, you may be going through a season of separation now, but if you remain faithful, God will elevate you to a position where you can save your family and bring them into God's blessing. It will require faith, endurance, and trust in God's timing because it is easy to get discouraged when the path is difficult, but remember that God's plan for your life is far bigger than you can see. You are not just enduring hardships for yourself; you are enduring them for the sake of your family and for generations to come. And like Joseph, when you look back on your life, you will be able to say, as written in Genesis 50:20,

"But as for you, ye thought evil against me; but God meant it unto good, to bring to pass, as it is this day, to save much people alive."

As you go through this process of separation and preparation, keep your eyes fixed on the promises of God. Declare that though your beginning is small, your latter end will significantly increase (Job 8:7). Embrace the grace for increase in every area of your life because your family's future depends on your ability to endure the process, stay faithful, and allow God to use you as His chosen vessel. I want you to know that separation is not a punishment but a necessary preparation process. Do not fight it; days will come when you are alone in your head, alone in your challenges, and you may feel like your trials are too much; however, always remember that "to whom much is given, much is also expected". You have a great destiny, so your training cannot be like that of others. Do not abort the process, go through it, and in the end, you will be glad you did.

Love Is A Command But Trust Is Not

"In being a blessing, you can love people blindly but not trust people blindly."

Forgive Your Family No Matter What

One critical lesson we must also learn from Joseph is the importance of forgiveness in this process. When Joseph's brothers came to Egypt during the famine, he could have harbored bitterness and resentment. And do you realize that Joseph could have easily killed all of them, and nobody would question him? These were the very same people God intended to save through him so that through them, the nation of Israel would rise, and through Israel, the savior would come, and we would all be saved, thereby fulfilling God's promise to Abraham, their Patriarch. Yet if Joseph had lacked the simple quality of being able to forgive all that God had been planning for maybe close to 400 years would have been destroyed.

But Joseph understood the bigger picture and he knew love had to prevail over vengeance because his suffering was not just about him but about God's plan to preserve his family. So, he forgave them (Genesis 45:5-7). Truly speaking, even for you, forgiveness is essential if you are to become the chosen vessel for your family's future. Holding on to bitterness or past hurts will only hinder you from fulfilling this God-given role. There are so many brothers who are bittered against their sisters, so many sisters bittered against their mothers, fathers are bittered against sons, and sons bittered against mothers, it does not matter what category of all these you fall into, you must correct it today. Go back home meet your family and make amends so that God's purposes would not be thwarted all to the detriment and destruction of your family.

The Balance Between Love And Trust

In this journey of becoming a blessing to others, particularly to your family, you also have to understand the delicate balance between love and trust. God commands us to love unconditionally in Matthew 22:39,

> *"And the second is like unto it, thou shalt love thy neighbour as thyself."*

This divine directive calls for a love that is blind to faults, shortcomings, and past transgressions. It is a love that reflects God's own nature, as described in 1 John 4:8 which says

> *"He that loveth not knoweth not God; for God is love."*

But then, although love is to be given freely and abundantly, trust is an entirely different matter. Trust is not commanded by God; rather, it is something that must be earned over time through consistent actions and proven character. This distinction is crucial for maintaining healthy relationships and protecting yourself from potential harm or continuous betrayal. Consider the example of Jesus himself, who, while loving all, did not entrust himself to everyone. John 2:24-25 says,

> *"But Jesus did not commit himself unto them, because he knew all men, and needed not that any should testify of man: for he knew what was in man."*

This truly shows us that even Jesus, in His perfect love, exercised discernment in trust.

Joseph who we have been discussing also did not blindly trust his brothers after forgiving them. He tested them to see if they had changed, as we see in Genesis 42:15-17. This should teach you that forgiveness does not necessarily mean blind trust, you can love your family deeply and forgive their past wrongs, but you must also have the wisdom to discern whether they have genuinely changed. In Joseph's case, He vetted them; he tested them and He gave them room to prove themselves because trust must be earned! He even took Benjamin their younger brother to see what they will do, but then Judah said, "No way! I'm not going*." This was when Joseph knew that yeas they could be trusted; he must have said in his heart "Really? Now I think I have my real brothers."* And then he revealed himself, saying, *"I am Joseph."*

This principle of loving blindly while being cautious with trust does not mean you have to become cynical or suspicious, it means you have to be careful in exercising wisdom as you deal with people especially those who may have already hurt you before. You must be mindful of who you allow into your inner circle and to whom you extend your trust. This is you recognizing that although you are called to love everyone including your enemies as stated in Matthew 5:44,

> *"But I say unto you, Love your enemies, bless them that curse you, do good to them that hate you, and pray for them which despitefully use you, and persecute you,"*

You are not obligated to trust everyone equally because trust has to be built over time especially through consistent actions that demonstrate reliability, integrity, and faithfulness.

CHAPTER SEVEN

DIVINE SEPARATION ALWAYS LEADS TO GLORY

◆ ◆ ◆

"Your willingness to separate from what holds you back is the key to unlocking the future God has planned for you."

◆ ◆ ◆

Learning From Abraham

The Power Of Saying Yes To God!

The journey of will faith often leads us through valleys of separation before we ascend to the mountaintops of glory. Just as we saw in the life of Joseph in the previous chapter, this mystery is also revealed in the life of Abraham, the patriarch of faith, whose story will forever be a wellspring of great lessons for us to learn from as far as the power of divine separation is concerned

Abraham's path of separation began with a call to from God in Genesis 12:1, where God commanded him,

> *"Now the Lord had said unto Abram, get thee out of thy country, and from thy kindred, and from thy father's house, unto a land that I will shew thee."*

This divine directive is what marked the beginning of a separation that ultimately led to unimaginable glory and blessing. You really need to never forget that God's call to separation is never without a course, it is always purposeful; when God separates us, He always does so with an intent and that intent is an intention to elevate us, purify us, bless us and position us for the fulfillment of His Plans. Isaiah 48:10 captures what happens in separation by saying,

> *"Behold, I have refined thee, but not with silver; I have chosen thee in the furnace of affliction."*

This scripture reveals that the process of separation, though often tough, is the crucible in which our faith is refined and our character is molded so that we can accurately host and also be able to administrate God's blessings which he intends to release on our lives.

Now let's talk about Abraham's obedience to God's call, I can assure you that it was not a very easy thing, and this is because he had to leave behind the familiarity of his homeland, the comfort of his family, and the security of his father's house, indeed it was a separation that required tremendous faith and courage. Yet, it was through this very act of obedience that Abraham positioned himself to receive God's unprecedented blessings.

The glory that follows divine separation is clearly seen in God's promises to Him. In Genesis 12:2-3, God said to him,

"And I will make of thee a great nation, and I will bless thee, and make thy name great; and thou shalt be a blessing: And I will bless them that bless thee, and curse him that curseth thee: and in thee shall all families of the earth be blessed."

Wow, what a great promise, these promises encompass not only personal blessings but also a far-reaching impact that would touch all of humanity.

A Deeper Examination

In examining his life even deeper, you will see how his separation led to a series of tests and trials that were all designed to strengthen his faith and prepare him for the glory destined for him. The journey to the Promised Land, the famine that drove him to Egypt, the separation from Lot, and the long wait for the promised heir were all part of God's refining process. Many people would probably have cursed and forsaken God today if they had to endure half of what he went through, but nevertheless, he went through it faithfully because he knew the end would greatly be an end of blessings and increase even though the beginning was small, challenging, and demanding.

Perhaps, the most poignant example of separation leading to glory in Abraham's life is found in the account of Isaac's near-sacrifice. In Genesis 22, God commanded Abraham to offer his son Isaac as a burnt offering. Do not forget, this was the very same son for whom Abraham waited years of his life to receive, the very same son for which even though his body was dead he had to refuse considering it, the very same son whom he loved with all his heart and God knew that Abraham loved this boy with all his heart.

Let us read the command in Genesis 22:1-2:

"And it came to pass after these things, that God did tempt Abraham, and said unto him, Abraham: and he said, Behold, here I am. And he said, Take now thy son, thine only son Isaac, whom thou lovest, and get thee into the land of Moriah; and offer him there for a burnt offering upon one of the mountains which I will tell thee of."

Can you see how God emphasized it, he said *"thy son"* that was not enough He then said *"thine only son"* it still wants enough, He then said *"whom thou lovest"*. Oh God! This is where any people would have said "hey! Enough! I will not do it" But not Abraham, He knew that if he was going to step into glory then he must be separated from everything, even Isaac his son. Indeed, this heart-breaking test required Abraham to separate himself from his most precious possession, his long-awaited son of promise. Yet, it was through this supreme act of faith and obedience that Abraham's covenant with God was irrevocably sealed.

After Abraham demonstrated his willingness to sacrifice Isaac, God intervened and provided a ram as a substitute. Then, in Genesis 22:16-18, God reaffirms His covenant with Abraham, saying,

"By myself have I sworn, saith the Lord, for because thou hast done this thing, and hast not withheld thy son, thine only son: That in blessing I will bless thee, and in multiplying I will multiply thy seed as the stars of the heaven, and as the sand which is upon the sea shore; and thy seed shall possess the gate of his enemies; And in thy seed shall all the nations of the earth be blessed; because thou hast obeyed my voice."

This powerful declaration shows us the principle that separation, when embraced in obedience to God, invariably leads to unprecedented blessing and glory. Abraham's willingness to separate himself from everything, even his beloved son, ultimately positioned him to receive a blessing that would impact all of humanity even till tomorrow.

The pattern of separation leading to glory is not unique to Abraham. Throughout Scripture, we see this principle at work in the lives of numerous biblical figures. Joseph endured separation from his family and years of imprisonment before rising to a position of power that enabled him to save nations. Moses spent forty years in the wilderness before leading the Israelites out of bondage. David experienced years of exile before ascending to the throne of Israel.

My Admonition To You

For us today, the call to separation may take various forms, it may involve leaving behind destructive habits, severing toxic relationships, or even stepping out of our comfort zones to follow God's leading; It may also require us to separate ourselves from worldly pursuits to focus on spiritual growth, or to let go of our plans and ambitions so as to effectively embrace and accept God's purpose for our lives. But regardless of the form it takes, I bring you good news that divine separation is always an invitation to greater intimacy with God and a pathway to His glorious blessings. When you yield to this process, you are positioning yourself to truly experience a life that is blessed and you will indeed experience the fullness of God's blessings and become a vessel through which His glory will be manifested to the world.

In Genesis 13:2, we see that *"Abram was very rich in cattle, in silver, and in gold."* This prosperity did not happen overnight, but it was the result of Abraham's obedience to God's call of separation. Another key lesson to learn from Abraham's life is that separation can lead to an increase. In Genesis 17:4-5, God changed Abram's name to Abraham, saying, *"As for me, behold, my covenant is with thee, and thou shalt be a father of many nations. Neither shall thy name anymore be called Abram, but thy name shall be Abraham; for a father of many nations have I made thee."* This change of name signifies a new identity and a new level of responsibility which indicates that Abraham's separation from his past was not just about leaving behind physical places; it was about stepping into a new identity and calling.

Truly, when God separates you, it is because He wants to increase your influence, your capacity, and your impact. But that increase requires leaving behind the old you because you cannot step into the new while holding on to the past. Like Abraham, we must all be willing to trust God and leave behind what is comfortable in order to step into the greater things He has for us. Abraham did not even have all the details when God called him to separate himself. He did not know exactly where he was going or what the journey would look like, but he trusted God and so he went. In line with this, I want you to know that faith is essential in the process of separation, you may not always have all the answers, but if you trust God, He will lead you to the place of glory and a realm of life where you become blessed beyond human reasoning's.

I beseech you today, if God is calling you to separate from something or someone do not resist it, instead, embrace the process, knowing that it is leading you to a place of great blessings and glory. The separation may be painful, but the outcome will be worth it. Just as Abraham's obedience resulted in generational blessings, your obedience can unlock blessings for your family and future generations so trust the process and know that God can be trusted.

A Practical Guide To Effectively Yielding To God's Separation And Some Pitfalls To Avoid

Revelations From Abraham's Life

When God calls you to separate, it is crucial to understand how to yield to that process effectively. Abraham's life offers valuable insights into how we can navigate this journey successfully. Here are five practical guides based on Abraham's life:

- **Embrace Immediate Obedience:**

One of the most striking aspects of Abraham's response to God's call is his immediate obedience. Genesis 12:4 tells us,

> *"So Abram departed, as the Lord had spoken unto him; and Lot went with him: and Abram was seventy and five years old when he departed out of Haran."*

There was no hesitation, negotiation, or delay in Abraham's response to God's command. This obedience is essential when yielding to God's call for separation. It demonstrates our trust in God's wisdom and timing and prevents us from being swayed by doubts or external influences. One thing that is clear through immediate obedience is that it reveals our willingness to prioritize God's will over our own comfort or plans. This may mean making difficult decisions quickly, leaving behind the familiar without delay, or stepping into new roles or responsibilities without hesitation. By embracing immediate obedience, you position yourself to receive the full blessings that God intends through our separation.

- **Walk by Faith, Not by Sight**

His faith in God's promises characterized Abraham's life of separation. The Bible says in Hebrews 11:8-10,

> *"By faith Abraham, when he was called to go out into a place which he should after receive for an inheritance, obeyed; and he went out, not knowing whither he went. By faith, he sojourned in the land of promise, as in a strange*

country, dwelling in tabernacles with Isaac and Jacob, the heirs with him of the same promise: For he looked for a city which hath foundations, whose builder and maker is God."

This strong faith is what enabled Abraham to persist in his journey of separation, even when the fulfillment of God's promises seemed distant and impossible.

To effectively yield to God's separation, you must begin to cultivate a similar faith, one that holds firm to God's promises even in the face of challenges, delays, or seeming contradictions. Romans 4:20-21 further describes Abraham's faith by saying

"He staggered not at the promise of God through unbelief; but was strong in faith, giving glory to God; And being fully persuaded that, what he had promised, he was able also to perform."

This kind of steadfast faith is what you need for effectively steering through the often challenging life of separation that God calls us to.

- **Maintain an Attitude of Worship**

Throughout his journey, Abraham maintained an attitude of worship and obedience. Genesis 12:7 shows that after God spoke to Abraham, *"he built an altar unto the LORD, who appeared unto him."* Worship is a critical part of yielding to God's separation because when we worship, we acknowledge God's sovereignty and remind ourselves that He is in control.

- **Stay Focused on the Promise, Not the Process**

The separation process can be challenging so it is important to stay focused on the promise rather than the difficulties along the way. God promised Abraham that he would be the father of many nations, even though Abraham did not have any children at the time. In Genesis 15:5, God told Abraham, *"Look now toward heaven, and tell the stars, if thou be able to number them: and he said unto him, so shall thy seed be."* This promise seemed impossible in the natural, but Abraham chose to focus on God's promise rather than the impossibility of his situation. When God calls you to separate, keep your eyes on His promises, knowing that He is faithful to fulfill them.

• Maintain a Godward Focus

Throughout his life of separation, Abraham maintained a consistent focus on God, and this is seen in his habit of building altars and calling on the name of the Lord wherever he went. Genesis 12:7-8 tells us

> *"And the Lord appeared unto Abram, and said, unto thy seed will I give this land: and there builded he an altar unto the Lord, who appeared unto him. And he removed from thence unto a mountain on the east of Bethel, and pitched his tent, having Bethel on the west, and Hai on the east: and there he builded an altar unto the Lord, and called upon the name of the Lord."*

This practice of regularly acknowledging God's presence and seeking His guidance is very important when yielding to divine separation. It will help you to remember the purpose behind your separation and keep you in with God's will. In our own lives, maintaining a Godward focus could mean establishing regular times of prayer and worship, consistently seeking God's guidance in our decisions, and intentionally acknowledging His presence in our daily activities; through doing all these, you definitely will be able to steer through the complexities of separation with grace and confidence.

• Be Patient and Wait on God's Timing

Another challenging aspect of yielding to God's separation is waiting on His timing. For example, Abraham waited many years for the fulfillment of God's promise, and David was anointed King when he was just a young boy, but did they see the manifestations immediately? NO! What this means is that patience is critical in this process.

• Maintain an Eternal Perspective

Abraham's ability to yield effectively to God's separation was also rooted in his eternal perspective toward life, the bible says in Hebrews 11:10 that Abraham *"looked for a city which hath foundations, whose builder and maker is God."* It was this focus on the eternal promises of God that enabled him to hold loosely to temporal comforts and security. When yielding to God's call for separation, maintaining an eternal perspective is of vital important because it will help you prioritize God's kingdom purposes over temporary gains or losses. Colossians 3:2

"Set your affection on things above, not on things on the earth."

When you keep your minds fixed on eternal realities, you can more readily embrace the changes and challenges that come with divine separation, knowing that they are contributing to an eternal weight of glory.

Now that we have discussed the guidelines that will help yield to God's call of separation, it is also very important to be aware of the pitfalls that can hinder your progress, so let us consider some of them

Some Pitfalls To Avoid

• The Pitfall of Partial Obedience

Although Abraham's life is largely characterized by obedience, there were moments when he fell into the trap of partial obedience. One of such instances is recorded in Genesis 12:1, where God instructs Abraham to leave his country, his people, and his father's household. However, Genesis 11:31 reveals that Abraham initially left Ur with his father Terah, and settled in Haran. It was not until after Terah's death that Abraham fully complied with God's original instruction. This delay in complete obedience serves as a cautionary revelation to us that partial obedience can often masquerade as full compliance, thereby leading us to believe we are following God's will when in reality we are holding back in certain areas.

This subtle form of compromise often hinders the full manifestation of God's blessings in our lives. To avoid this pitfall, you must cultivate thorough obedience, carefully examining your heart and actions to ensure you do not subconsciously resist God's instructions in any area. 1 Samuel 15:22

> "Behold, to obey is better than sacrifice, and to hearken than the fat of rams."

Actual separation requires a wholehearted commitment to God's directives, so stop trying to bargain God's directives and start complying in complete obedience.

· The Pitfall of Fear-Driven Decisions

Despite his great faith, Abraham occasionally succumbed to fear, leading to decisions that compromised his integrity and almost jeopardized God's plan. A prime example of this is found in Genesis 12:10-20 and again in Genesis 20, where Abraham, fearing for his life, presented his wife Sarah as his sister. This deception, born out of fear, not only put Sarah in a precarious position but also risked derailing God's promise of an heir through her. This should always remind you of allowing fear to dictate your actions, especially during your seasons of separation and testing.

Fear can cloud your judgment, cause you to doubt God's protection, provision, and lead you to rely on your own devices rather than trust in God's faithfulness. To avoid this pitfall, you must actively combat your fear with faith by continually reminding yourself of God's good character and His proven track record of faithfulness. You can meditate on verses like Isaiah 41:10

"Fear thou not; for I am with thee: be not dismayed; for I am thy God: I will strengthen thee; yea, I will help thee; yea, I will uphold thee with the right hand of my righteousness."

By anchoring yourself in God's word and cultivating a deep trust in His character, you will be able to resist the urge to make fear-driven decisions that will compromise your integrity and hinder God's work in your lives.

- ### Looking Back

Another pitfall to avoid is looking back to what you've left behind, when God called Abraham to separate, He told him to leave everything behind and move forward. In Genesis 19:26, we see the consequences of looking back when Lot's wife turned into a pillar of salt because she looked back at Sodom. Once God calls you to separate, do not long for the past, just keep moving forward in faith and letting go of the old so you can fully embrace the new.

In a nutshell, as you continually navigate your journey of separation, you should always prioritize drawing close to Godin this season. I pray that, like Abraham, you will be found faithful in your response to God's call, trusting in His promises, and leaving a legacy that impacts generations to come.

CHAPTER EIGHT

THE BLESSING MAKES YOU A MENTOR

❖ ❖ ❖

"Your blessings are not just for you; they are meant to flow through you to empower and inspire those around you."

❖ ❖ ❖

Principles For Being A Blessed Mentor

Understanding How The Blessing Makes You A Mentor

As the Lord begins to elevate you in your walk with Him, He will also simultaneously bring people to be nurtured under your spiritual tutelage. These are souls that have been divinely appointed to benefit from your guidance, wisdom, and experience, people whom you are called to mentor and shepherd toward their own God-ordained destiny.

You should know that this mentorship role is a delicate by-product of being blessed because it is in the very nature of God's blessings to multiply, as we have been reading in Genesis 12:2. In this verse have you observed how the Lord's promise to Abraham is meant to effortlessly transition from a personal blessing to becoming a blessing for others? This is the same divine principle that applies to all who walk in the blessing of the Lord, the moment you become blessed you now have a responsibility of guiding others into the blessings of the Lord. You really should understand that this mentorship role is never to be taken lightly. If you fail to master the art of godly mentorship, there lies a grave danger of inadvertently destroying and bringing harm to the very lives the Lord has entrusted to your care; this is why James 3:1 will caution us by saying,

> *"My brethren, be not many masters, knowing that we shall receive the greater condemnation."*

This is a cautionary reminder of the weighty responsibility that comes with spiritual leadership and mentorship. If you fail to mentor the people under you well, if you end up destroying their lives rather than helping them achieve destiny, then you can be sure a grave punishment awaits you in eternity.

To truly flourish as a mentor, you must cultivate a deep understanding of God's ways and His heart for His children and this understanding is not just intellectual in nature but also experiential, born out of a close walk with the Lord and a willingness to be continually shaped by His hand (Proverbs 9:10). Also, effective mentorship will require that you genuinely have a genuine love for those under your care so that you can mirror the love of Christ for His church through the way you relate with them. This love would manifest in patience, kindness, and a sincere desire to see them become blessed, succeed, and even surpass their own achievements.

In essence, being a blessed mentor is about becoming a conduit of God's grace, wisdom, love, and a map through which others can step into the blessings of the Lord.

11 Keys To Being A Blessing As A Mentor:

Learn to Inspire Confidence in Others

As a blessed mentor, one of your primary responsibilities is to inspire confidence in those under your guidance and tutelage. I am talking about being able to help them reach the point of greatly believing in their God-given potential because your words and actions can serve as a mirror, reflecting the image of Christ in them, helping them see themselves as God sees them, and eventually getting them to a point where they know they are destined for greatness.

In the book of Numbers, we see a powerful example of this principle in action. When Moses sent twelve spies to scout the Promised Land, only Joshua and Caleb returned with a report full of faith and confidence. Their words in Numbers 13:30 were,

> *"And Caleb stilled the people before Moses, and said, let us go up at once, and possess it; for we are well able to overcome it."*

This declaration of confidence, rooted in faith in God's promises, stood in stark contrast to the fear-filled report of the other spies. As a mentor, your role is to be like Caleb, instilling confidence in the face of seemingly insurmountable odds. In line with this, you must also learn to demonstrate faith in God's ability to work through those you mentor; when you can have faith in them, they will also have faith in themselves because through you, they can see beyond their current limitations and into the realm of divine possibilities.

Also, inspiring confidence will mean creating an environment where failure is not seen as final, but as a stepping stone to success, Proverbs 24:16 says, *"For a just man falleth seven times, and riseth up again."* By creating an environment of resilience and perseverance, you are equipping your mentees to bounce back from setbacks, and always growing stronger with each challenge they face.

Govern and Control Yourself

The cornerstone of effective leadership and mentorship lies in the ability to exercise self-control. As a blessed mentor, you must first master the art of governing yourself before you can hope to guide others; this is a principle that can be clearly and beautifully seen in Proverbs 16:32, which states, *"He that is slow to anger is better than the mighty; and he that ruleth his spirit than he that taketh a city."* Self-governance encompasses every aspect of your life such as your thoughts, words, actions, and even your reactions to circumstances beyond your control. It involves cultivating discipline in your spiritual life, maintaining integrity in your dealings, and exhibiting emotional stability even in the face of provocation or adversity.

Think about the example of David, who, despite having the opportunity to slay King Saul in the cave of En-gedi, chose to exercise restraint. His words in 1 Samuel 24:6 reveal the depth of his self-control:

> *"And he said unto his men, The Lord forbid that I should do this thing unto my master, the Lord's anointed, to stretch forth mine hand against him, seeing he is the anointed of the Lord."*

This act of self-governance not only preserved David's integrity but also set a powerful example for those who followed him. As a mentor, your ability to control yourself will be constantly put to the test. There will be times when you're tempted to react in anger, to speak hastily, or to compromise your principles for short-term gain. In these moments, remember the words of Galatians 5:22-23:

"But the fruit of the Spirit is love, joy, peace, longsuffering, gentleness, goodness, faith, Meekness, temperance: against such there is no law."

By consistently demonstrating self-control, you safeguard your walk with God and provide a living example for those you mentor to emulate. Your life becomes a testament to the transformative power of God's grace, inspiring others to pursue a life of disciplined devotion to the Lord.

Master the Art of Decision-Making

As a blessed mentor, you must never forget that one of your most important and very vital responsibilities is to master the art of decision-making, this skill is not just about choosing between right and wrong, but about discerning God's will in every situation, regardless of popular opinion or personal comfort. The foundation of godly decision-making is rooted in a deep understanding and application of God's Word. Proverbs 3:5-6 provides an instruction that will help you with this *"Trust in the Lord with all thine heart; and lean not unto thine own understanding. In all thy ways acknowledge him, and he shall direct thy paths."* This is a scripture emphasizing the importance of surrendering our own limited understanding to the infinite wisdom of God because it is only through surrendering that we can tap into his knowledge and use it to change lives.

Think of Joshua for example, who faced the monumental decision of how to conquer Jericho. Instead of relying on conventional military tactics, he sought the Lord's guidance and followed His unconventional strategy, resulting in a miraculous victory (Joshua 6:1-20). This teaches us in an amazing way about how godly decision-making often defies human logic but aligns with divine wisdom. As a mentor, you must cultivate the ability to hear God's voice amidst the clamor of conflicting opinions and worldly advice and this will demand from your consistent communion with God through prayer and meditation on His Word (Psalm 119:105). By consistently making decisions based on God's Word and leading, you are also setting a powerful example for those you mentor and demonstrating that true wisdom and success come not from conforming to worldly standards, but from aligning our choices with God's perfect will.

Be Reliable

Reliability is a cornerstone of effective mentorship and leadership. As a blessed mentor, your dependability should reflect God's unwavering faithfulness. Proverbs 25:19 shows us the importance of reliability by saying *"Confidence in an unfaithful man in time of trouble is like a broken tooth, and a foot out of joint."* This clearly shows us the pain and disappointment caused by unreliability. Reliability means being consistent in your words and actions, following through on your commitments, and being a steady presence in the lives of those you mentor. It also involves being punctual, honoring your promises, and maintaining a high standard of integrity in all your dealings. Daniel was indeed a great example of this; he was a man whose reliability was so renowned that even his enemies could find no fault in him. Daniel 6:4:

> *"Then the presidents and princes sought to find occasion against Daniel concerning the kingdom; but they could find none occasion nor fault; forasmuch as he was faithful, neither was there any error or fault found in him."*

Daniel's faithfulness to God translated into reliability in his earthly duties and set him apart as a man of excellence.

Being a mentor, know that your reliability creates a safe environment for growth and learning by building trust in your mentees, and this is very essential for effective mentorship. When those under your guidance know they can count on you, they are more likely to open up, seek advice, and implement the wisdom you share. This reliability must extend to your spiritual life.

Handle Contrary Situations

As a blessed mentor, developing the ability to navigate contradictions and stand firm in the face of challenges is crucial. Life is filled with ups and downs, and your resilience in these moments will serve as a powerful example to those you are mentoring and guiding. Handling contrary situations will mean maintaining a positive outlook even when circumstances seem dire and holding fast to God's promises when everything around you seem to contradict them. Do you remember when Moses, in Exodus 14:13-15, faced the seemingly impossible situation of being trapped between Pharaoh's army and the Red Sea? His response shows how to handle contrary situations:

"And Moses said unto the people, Fear ye not, stand still, and see the salvation of the Lord, which he will shew to you today: for the Egyptians whom ye have seen today, ye shall see them again no more forever. The Lord shall fight for you, and ye shall hold your peace."

As a mentor, you must teach those under your guidance that their friends or circumstances are not the ones who will fight their battles; God is! This truth is very loud in 2 Chronicles 20:15 *"Thus saith the Lord unto you, Be not afraid nor dismayed by reason of this great multitude; for the battle is not yours, but God's."*

By consistently demonstrating faith and courage in the face of contrary situations, you equip your mentees with the spiritual tools necessary to overcome their own challenges. You show them that with God, no problem is truly hopeless and that every trial is an opportunity for growth and for God's power to be manifested.

Lead Through Contradictions

In a world filled with confusion and contradictions, your role as a blessed mentor is to be a beacon of God's truth and wisdom. Leading through contradictions involves maintaining a clear vision of God's principles and purposes, even when the surrounding culture promotes conflicting values. This requires a deep understanding of God's Word and the courage to stand firm on its truths. Apostle Paul's exhortation in Romans 12:2 captures this principle for us:

> *"And be not conformed to this world: but be ye transformed by the renewing of your mind, that ye may prove what is that good, and acceptable, and perfect, will of God."*

As a mentor, you are called to influence your surroundings with God's ideas rather than being swayed by worldly philosophies. Daniel and his friends in Babylon. Despite being immersed in a culture that contradicted their faith, they were able to remain steadfast in their commitment to God. Daniel 1:8 says,

> *"But Daniel purposed in his heart that he would not defile himself with the portion of the king's meat, nor with the wine which he drank."*

Their stance not only preserved their integrity but also influenced the entire kingdom.

Leading through contradictions will also demand helping those you mentor discern truth from error. As 1 John 4:1 says, *"Beloved, believe not every spirit, but try the spirits whether they are of God:*

because many false prophets are gone out into the world."

Embrace Responsibility

As a blessed mentor, embracing responsibility is a duty and a divine calling. This means taking ownership of your actions, decisions, and consequences and accepting the responsibility for guiding and nurturing those under your care. Galatians 6:5 scripture shows us this principle: *"For every man shall bear his burden."* Embracing responsibility means stepping up to the challenges that come with leadership rather than shying away from them. It involves being accountable to those you lead and primarily to God. As we see in the parable of the talents (Matthew 25:14-30), God expects us to be good stewards of the gifts, abilities, and people He has entrusted to us.

Embracing responsibility also means being willing to admit mistakes and learn from them. This vulnerability creates an environment of authenticity and growth for those you lead. Also, embracing responsibility means proactively seeking ways to serve and uplift others. As Jesus taught in Mark 10:43-44,

> *"But so shall it not be among you: but whosoever will be great among you, shall be your minister: And whosoever of you will be the chiefest, shall be servant of all."*

By fully embracing your mentoring responsibilities, you model a life of integrity, servant leadership, and faithful stewardship. This honors God and inspires those you mentor to confidently and purposefully step into their God-given duties.

Communicate Effectively

Effective communication is the cornerstone of successful mentorship and leadership. So, as a blessed mentor, you must realize that your ability to articulate thoughts, feelings, and spiritual truths clearly and impactfully is essential, and you cannot bargain about this. The Bible says in Proverbs 25:11,

> *"A word fitly spoken is like apples of gold in pictures of silver."*

Effective communication goes beyond mere transmission of information; it involves ensuring understanding, fostering connection, and inspiring action. It requires speaking with clarity and conviction and listening with empathy and discernment. As James 1:19 advises, *"Wherefore, my beloved brethren, let every man be swift to hear, slow to speak, slow to wrath."*

Think about the example of Jesus, who was the master communicator; He always used parables, questions, and object lessons to convey spiritual truths in ways that connected with His audience. For instance, when he was teaching about the Kingdom of God, how did he do it? He did not resort to complex theological arguments. Instead, He used everyday examples that His listeners could relate to, like the parable of the mustard seed in Matthew 13:31-32

> *"The kingdom of heaven is like to a grain of mustard seed, which a man took, and sowed in his field: Which indeed is the least of all seeds: but when it is grown, it is the greatest among herbs, and becometh a tree, so that the birds of the air come and lodge in the branches thereof."*

This approach made His teachings accessible and memorable, allowing His disciples to grasp and apply complex spiritual concepts daily.

As a mentor, you must learn to adapt your communication style to suit the needs and understanding of those you are mentoring; they will demand that you keep breaking down complex ideas into simpler terms, using relatable examples, or even employing visual aids when necessary. It is not just about imparting information but ensuring that the information is understood and can be applied practically. This ties in with the wisdom found in 1 Corinthians 9:22, where Paul says,

"To the weak became I as weak, that I might gain the weak: I am made all things to all men, that I might by all means save some."

While Paul was referring to evangelism, the principle applies equally to mentorship, we must be willing to adapt our approach to reach and teach those under our guidance effectively.

Do not forget that communication is a two-way street; as vital as it is to speak clearly and effectively, it is equally crucial to be an active listener. This means giving your full attention when others are talking, seeking to understand their perspective, and responding thoughtfully rather than reactively. James 1:19 emphasizes this, saying, *"Wherefore, my beloved brethren, let every man be swift to hear, slow to speak, slow to wrath."* By practicing active listening, you gain valuable insights into the needs and challenges of those you're mentoring and model an essential skill for them to develop in their leadership journey.

Also, as a mentor, your communication should always be rooted in love and aimed at building up those you're guiding. Ephesians 4:29 provides a powerful guideline:

"Let no corrupt communication proceed out of your mouth, but that which is good to the use of edifying, that it may minister grace unto the hearers."

This means that even when correction or criticism is necessary, it should be delivered with kindness to help the other person grow.

Cultivate Empathy:

Empathy is also a vital quality for any mentor who wishes to truly understand and train those under their guidance effectively; this is about putting yourself in someone else's shoes so you can feel what they feel and see the world from their perspective. It does not mean you always agree with them, but it truly means that you sincerely try to understand their point of view. Romans 12:15:

> *"Rejoice with them that do rejoice, and weep with them that weep."*

Do you get it? As a mentor, cultivating empathy will allow you to connect with your mentees on a deeper level. It can help you recognize their struggles, celebrate their victories, and even provide significant support. This may not always be easy, but you do not have a choice, especially when dealing with people whose experiences or perspectives differ significantly from yours. God expects you to do an excellent job with them.

When you look at the life of Jesus, you will see that he consistently demonstrated empathy throughout His earthly ministry. When He encountered the woman at the well in John 4, He did not condemn her for her, past. Instead, He engaged her in conversation, understood her situation, and offered her living water; this opened the door for a life-changing encounter. Cultivating empathy will require patience with those struggling or making mistakes. Do not forget that everyone's journey is different, and what comes easily to you may be a significant challenge for someone else.

Promote Collaboration:

As a blessed mentor, creating a spirit of collaboration among those you are called to lead is very important for their growth and the overall success of your mentorship. What does collaboration indeed mean? Collaboration is not just about working together; it is about creating a conducive environment where diverse talents and perspectives can come together to achieve common goals. Ecclesiastes 4:9-10 puts it this way:

"Two are better than one; because they have a good reward for their labor. If they fall, the one will lift his fellow: but woe to him that is alone when he falleth; for he hath not another to help him up."

In truth, as far as life is concerned, no one person has all the answers or abilities; we all must always humbly acknowledge that we need each other to reach our full potential in Christ. The Apostle Paul uses the metaphor of the body to explain this concept in 1 Corinthians 12:14-27, emphasizing how each part, though different, is essential for the functioning of the whole.

As a mentor, you can create opportunities for your mentees to work together on projects or solve problems as a team, teaching them to pray together, study together, etc. This will help them learn from each other and prepare them for the collaborative nature of most real-world environments. Also, you should be available to guide these collaborations to ensure that everyone can contribute and that the group stays focused on its goals. In promoting cooperation, you will also need to teach your mentees how to steer through differences in opinion and resolve conflicts godly; this can be done by encouraging an atmosphere of mutual respect, honest communication, and a willingness to consider people's viewpoints. They should never forget Philippians 2:3-4:

"Let nothing be done through strife or vainglory, but in lowliness of mind let each esteem other better than, themselves. Look not every man on his things, but every man also on the things of others."

The goal of collaboration in mentorship is to accomplish tasks more efficiently and create a community of believers who support and uplift each other in their spiritual and personal growth. As you promote collaboration, you're helping to build the kind of unity that Jesus prayed for in John 17:21:

> *"That they all may be one; as thou, Father, art in me, and I in thee, that they also may be one in us: that the world may believe that thou hast sent me."*

Stay Humble:

I genuinely love Proverbs 11:2, which says,

> *"When pride cometh, then cometh shame: but with the lowly is wisdom."*

Humility is the cornerstone of effective mentoring and leadership. As a blessed mentor, you must never forget that your position is a gift from God, not a reason for pride or self-importance. This demonstrates to us the value of remaining modest in your mentoring role. Now, I would like you to know and never forget that staying humble does not mean downplaying your abilities or the wisdom God has given you; that will be false humility; what it means is that you recognize that these gifts are from God and are intended to be used in service to others, not for self-aggrandizement. 1 Peter 4:10 tells us that

> *"As every man hath received the gift, even so minister the same one to another, as good stewards of the manifold grace of God."*

Do you remember John the Baptist? He is a shining example of this because, despite his significant role in preparing the way for Jesus, he maintained a posture of humility and even said of Jesus in John 3:30, *"He must increase, but I must decrease."* This attitude allowed John to fulfill his calling without letting pride or ego get in the way.

So, child of God, as a mentor, you must be humble, and this also means being open to learning from those you are guiding, acknowledging when you do not have all the answers, and being willing to grow alongside your mentees. Humility also has to do with being willing to admit your mistakes and ask for forgiveness when necessary; as a matter of fact, this will not only model integrity for your mentees but also create a safe space for them to be honest about their struggles and shortcomings.

You Are In Charge Because Of The Blessing

In Luke 8:22-24, we have a moment filled with contradiction and chaos. What happened was that the wind and the waves were threatening to sink the ship through which the Lord was crossing over alongside his disciples, yet Jesus was peacefully asleep beneath the deck. Before we knew it, His disciples became overwhelmed with fear and quickly rushed to wake Him, crying out, *"Master, Master, we are perishing!"* The most fantastic thing for me in this scripture was Jesus's response. He was so calm, relaxed, and undisturbed. When he finally came up, He rebuked the wind and the raging waves, saying, *"Peace be still,"* immediately, everything became still. Do you see authority at work? This is the power of being in charge! See, when the blessings of God are at work in your life, I tell you the truth: you can remain unshakeable amidst life's storms.

The disciples were terrified, but Jesus was in control! Here's what you should catch now: "The blessing gives you power, and it gives you the authority to navigate the surprises and challenges life throws your way."

If you face unexpected challenges, I declare in the name of Jesus that every challenging surprise waiting for you as you journey through life will be silenced in the name of Jesus."

Just as Jesus calmed the storm, I declare over your life that the winds and storms will subside in the name of Jesus... I speak to every spiritual storm, every cloud of confusion, every bit of oppression and depression, as well as bad dreams and nightmares that torment you, and I command them to cease by the mercies of God.

I may not be completely aware of what you are going through right now, but as long as God's blessings are at work in your life, no storms can sink you because the blessing of the Lord makes you unsinkable!

The response of Jesus is instructive and inspiring; His actions demonstrate the authority that comes with God's blessing. I am emphasizing this again because I need it to sink in your heart that you have this same authority. Did Jesus panic? Then, you must not panic in your storms. Did he become filled with anxiety? Then, you must also reject anxiety in your stormy days. What did he do with calm assurance? He simply spoke and rebuked the wind and the raging waves. This is what you should be doing! You should be rebuking your storms with the authority of God over your life, not crying and making those storms and situations feel more significant than your God! The Greek word used here for *"rebuke"* is the same word used in the Gospels when Jesus commanded demons to be silent. This linguistic parallel tells us that Jesus was exercising authority not just over natural elements but over spiritual forces as well. And do you know the beautiful part? You can do the same. After the command, the storm did not gradually subside; it instantly obeyed the voice of its Creator. This dramatic demonstration of authority serves as a powerful reminder of the truth declared in Colossians 1:16-17:

"For by him were all things created, that are in heaven, and that are in earth, visible and invisible, whether they be thrones, or dominions, or principalities, or powers: all things were created by him, and for him: And he is before all things, and by him all things consist."

Will you not start using your authority today? Will you not begin commanding Today? What are you waiting for?

Being people who have the Lord has blessed us, we are called to emulate Christ's example in our spheres of influence; what this means is that you should stop praying for challenges not to come. Instead, you should realize that when you face challenges, you have the authority to face them with faith and confidence, knowing that the same God who calmed the storm now lives in you and has filled you with his authority. This revelation unapologetically revolutionizes your approach to the surprises and challenges that life inevitably brings. Instead of being paralyzed by fear or overwhelmed by your circumstances, begin to exercise the authority given to you through God's blessing. Yes, you can speak peace to the storms in your life, whether relational conflicts, financial difficulties, health challenges, or any other form of adversity. Do you remember the words of Isaiah 54:17:

"No weapon that is formed against thee shall prosper; and every tongue that shall rise against thee in judgment thou shalt condemn. This is the heritage of the servants of the Lord, and their righteousness is of me, saith the Lord."

This is an assurance that no attack formed against you can succeed.

So, next time you face challenges, what should you do? Declare with confidence, *"I am unsinkable!"* by this declaration, you recognize the power of God's blessing working in your life.

CHAPTER NINE

YOUR TIME IS NOW

♦ ♦ ♦

"Let your mind dwell on the increase because you are destined for greatness beyond your current circumstances."

♦ ♦ ♦

IT WON'T BE LONG

As we gradually reach the end of this book, know that the Lord has a word for you today: *"Your time of being blessed is NOW!"* No matter the situation or how long you may have been waiting, I want you to key into this: God is saying that your breakthrough is closer than you think. You may have endured years of struggles, setbacks, and delays, but now is the time to open your heart to the overflowing blessings God has in store for you. Amos 9:13 (Message Translation) says,

"Yes indeed, it won't be long now. God's decree: things will happen so fast your head will swim. One thing fast on the heels of the other."

This scripture is filled with prophetic insights urging us to understand that God's blessings are not just coming for you; they are coming fast. Yes, begin confidently declaring to people that *"It won't be long now!"* Believe it and say it with faith because God's timing is perfect, and He is ready to accelerate the fulfillment of His promises in your life.

Perhaps you have been feeling weighed down by your current circumstances. Well, right now, God is reminding you that He is not bound by delays, and your blessings are on their way swiftly. Yes, *"Good things are coming!"* I want you to boldly declare these words right now: *"I am blessed to be a blessing!"*

Imagine if God had told Abraham that he would have a child, and two years later, Isaac was born. If the promise had been fulfilled so quickly, there would have been no need for Abraham and Sarah to create an alternative plan, which resulted in the birth of Ishmael. Still, because they grew weary of waiting, they took matters into their own hands, and this is often the trap we fall into when delays push us into impatience. Know this: Delays are the enemy's tactic to try us out of alignment with God's perfect timing. But today, I declare that any agent or circumstance causing delays in the manifestation of God's promises in your life is terminated in the name of Jesus!

Think about this: when you drink water, what happens? It refreshes, right? How about when you take honey? It brings sweetness and satisfaction. While water is good, it does not compare to the richness and sweetness of honey; this is a challenge for many people. In the delay, we often settle for water when God is preparing honey. If Sarah had waited for the honey of Isaac instead of settling for the water of delay, Ishmael would never have entered the picture, talk less of the troubles he brought to her and continues to bring to the world. Sometimes, we create Ishmaels in our lives; these are the temporary fixes that seem right at the moment but later create challenges for us all because we weren't patient enough to wait for the sweetness of God's promise.

Amos 9:13 continues, *"You won't be able to keep up! Everything will be happening at once!"* This is the nature of divine acceleration; when God decides to bless you, it is not in drips or drops; it is in floods. One blessing will come right after the other, and another will appear before you can recover from one testimony. This is the type of outpouring you need to expect. Whether financial breakthroughs, health miracles, or testimonies that amaze people, God is ready to elevate you swiftly. His plan for you is to break free from every form of delay, poverty, sickness, and setback. And when it happens, it won't just be a trickle but a deluge of blessings.

Child of God, stay hooked up to the lord; your increase is inevitable if you align yourself with God's purpose. Psalm 115:14 says,

> *"The Lord shall increase you more and more, you and your children."*

This is a promise for you and your descendants, and I want you to declare it out loud: *"The Lord is increasing me!".* You must start thinking about the increase right now; stop thinking about lack, want, poverty, struggles, and all kinds of negativity. Job 8:7 says,

> *"Though thy beginning was small, yet thy latter end should greatly increase."*

We have looked at this scripture a lot, so by now, it should be engraved in your heart, and you should be very confident that you will never end in a small way.

Let your mind dwell on verses like Psalm 71:21, which says, *"Thou shalt increase my greatness and comfort me on every side."* This is the promise of God to you, and it is pronounced: "Increase is part of your destiny." Zechariah 10:8 says,

> *"I will hiss for them, and gather them; for I have redeemed them: and they shall increase as they have increased."*

God is positioning you for explosive growth; you only need to accept this truth now.

Are you ready for your business to explode? Are you ready for opportunities to manifest suddenly in your life? You might feel unprepared, wondering if God is setting you up for failure, but do not worry; God has been preparing you for such a time as this; all those years of waiting and all those trials you have endured were God's way of getting you ready for this season of overflow. Satan may have spent years stealing from you, whether it was your joy, finances, or destiny, but right now, the Lord is declaring that it is time for restoration. And I decree that whatever you may have lost comes back to you in more significant measure in the name of Jesus. The enemy may have delayed your progress, but God is accelerating your restoration! Joel 2:25:

> *"And I will restore to you the years that the locust hath eaten, the cankerworm, the caterpillar, and the palmerworm, my great army which I sent among you."*

Blessings upon blessings are coming your way!

Whether you look to the north, south, east, or west, you will be blessed because your blessings are not confined to one area of your life; the Lord is bringing a holistic blessing that will cut through all areas.

Overflowing Blessings

Luke 6:38 says, "Give, and it shall be given unto you; good measure, pressed down, shaken together, and running over, shall men give into your bosom."

This reveals that the blessing of God comes in an overflowingly good measure, which is pressed down, shaken together, and spilling over. Sometimes, you can experience God's blessings and not even know it, so you need to be conscious of this dimension.

What do I mean? You see, Sometimes the blessings of God work to bring good things into your life, and at other times, they block bad things from coming in. You might not always understand why particular doors are closed or why some plans fail, but if you trust in God's goodness, you will see that even the *"no's"* are part of His protection. Imagine wanting to buy a house, but somehow the deal goes wrong, and the owner refuses to sell; you may be angry, but if you look with the eyes of the spirit, you may realize that God was only protecting you from some government troubles that may come up regarding the property in the future. You may be fighting for a business deal, but then someone steals the agreement from you; it is natural to feel sad, but if you look deeper, you may just realize it is God protecting you from being defrauded. Yes, that is precisely how God works. He expects you to trust him, so He does not have to come and explain every little thing to you in detail. This is why we walk and live by faith and trust in God, not by explanations from Him.

In essence, I am saying that even when things do not seem to go your way, remember that God's favor and blessings are upon you. The circumstances you face are often divine interventions rather than signs of divine disfavor because His blessings are tangible and protective. Learn to live by faith even when you do not understand because God can be trusted.

Corrections Keep You Stable And Thriving

As we slowly wrap up, I want to discuss a key component of maintaining and thriving in your blessings.

You have to develop the ability to receive correction! It does not matter how high you climb or how successful you become; if you cannot accept corrections, you are setting yourself up for a great fall. Proverbs 12:1 says

> *"Whoso loveth instruction loveth knowledge: but he that hateth reproof is brutish."*

I should probably start by letting you know that correction is not an attack on your value; it is God's way of keeping you in line with His purposes. Whether you are leading a household, a business, or a ministry, you must remain humble enough to receive correction from God and the people around you. Do not forget that pride is the enemy of progress, and if you refuse to be corrected, you are exposing yourself to mistakes, pitfalls, and even destruction. Abraham made mistakes, but he was open to God's correction, when he went ahead of God's plan by fathering Ishmael, God corrected him and still fulfilled His promise through Isaac. This means that God's correction does not disqualify you from His promises. Rather, it will help to ensure you are on the right path to receiving them.

One man who truly understood this was David, David made all kinds of mistakes, even beyond the mistakes of Saul, yet David remained under God's favor and blessings while Saul even shamefully lost his life, what was the difference between both of them? The difference is that David was always quick to accept his wrong, take correction, and then repent, whereas Saul was a man who always had an excuse, always seeking to justify his actions.

You should also know that sometimes, correction comes from unexpected sources, it could be a friend, a mentor, or even a spouse. The point is do not despise it no matter who is bringing it, even if it is your junior in ministry, a junior in the office, or junior siblings, just accept it and make swift amendments.

> *Proverbs 15:31: "The ear that heareth the reproof of life abideth among the wise."*

By accepting correction, you set yourself up for continuous growth and success. Being a leader in any capacity, I know that you want your blessings and influence to have a global impact, but do you know what? That will only happen if you remain teachable! Being teachable will keep you grounded, humble, and ready for every next level of growth. So, Child of God, work on this principle, be receptive to correction, and no matter how far you may have come or how much you may have achieved, remember that Proverbs 3:12 says,

> *"For whom the Lord loveth he correcteth; even as a father the son in whom he delighteth."*

CONCLUSION

After reading through this book, I want you to walk away with one truth: the revelation that *"the Lord has blessed you."* This is not just a vague or abstract statement; it is a divine reality that carries power. God's blessing upon your life will empower you to live above struggles, lack, and all, limitations the enemy may try to impose upon you. But it is not enough to know that you are blessed, you must also decide to take action based on this knowledge and everything you have now learned by reading this book. This is where many people miss it, "Knowledge without action is useless." The Bible is clear on this. James 1:22:

> *"But be ye doers of the word, and not hearers only, deceiving your selves".*

Every believer must understand this is a great truth because merely hearing or knowing the Word of God is not enough to bring about the transformation you desire in your life. You have learned that the blessings become activated in doing the Word and acting on the principles.

God's blessings are always accompanied by instruction, and when you carry out those instructions in obedience, you position yourself to experience the fullness of His promises. Let me put it this way, *"blessings follow obedience."* If you refuse to do the Word, no matter how much knowledge you have in your head, it will not yield results. I know many people who can quote scripture, attend church, and even teach others, some even probably won a bible competition at one point or the other in their life. But if they are not applying the Word in their daily lives, they will not see the manifestation of God's promises, and that's the truth!

> *Jesus said in Luke 11:28, "Blessed are they that hear the word of God, and keep it".*

It is clear that blessing comes not only from hearing but also from doing; to keep the word means TO DO IT and LIVE BY IT! Are you set to experience an increase in rapid succession? The Lord has already given you everything you need through Christ, but your actions and faith will determine whether you fully experience that blessing in your life.

There will be days when you do not understand why certain things are happening, and that's okay; this is why you must hold on to the promises of God. You must remember what God has said in the challenging moments rather than focusing on the challenges around you. His Word is always true, regardless of how things look.

> *Romans 8:28 says that "all things work together for good to them that love God, to them who are the called according to his purpose".*

Even when everything is falling apart, God is still working behind the scenes, turning things around for your benefit. So, when things do not make sense, do not give in to discouragement; stand firm in faith and believe that God's blessing is upon your life and that the blessing is working in you, through you, and for you.

Child of God, as you close up this book and step into the next season of your life, I want you to remember that the Lord blesses you. Do not just carry this knowledge in your head; live it out daily. Be a doer of the Word. And when challenges come, or you feel you are going down, pick the book again, go through it again, and let it renew your mind and strengthen your faith till you see your victory!

Let God's Word take root in your heart and produce a harvest of blessings in every area of your life.

God Bless you!

ABOUT THE BOOK

God has never intended that any of His children would live on the lower levels of life. His intention has always been that we will continually thrive and keep moving from one level of glory to another. However, we have so many believers who are finding life very difficult. Well, is God to be blamed? No! Our God is a caring and loving father who wants the best for all of us. Many are having things so bad because they do not understand that they have been blessed to increase and those who do, are not yet knowledgeable on how to activate these blessings in their lives. This book is a compendium of God's wisdom, which is meant to hold your hands and walk you through the principles you need to understand so that you can begin to live the life God intended for you to live.

www.ingramcontent.com/pod-product-compliance
Lightning Source LLC
Chambersburg PA
CBHW071857020426
42331CB00010B/2561